Bridging the 'Know–Do' Gap

Knowledge brokering to improve child wellbeing

Bridging the 'Know–Do' Gap

Knowledge brokering to improve child wellbeing

Edited by Gabriele Bammer with
Annette Michaux and Ann Sanson

ANU
THE AUSTRALIAN NATIONAL UNIVERSITY

E PRESS

ANU

E PRESS

Published by ANU E Press
The Australian National University
Canberra ACT 0200, Australia
Email: anuepress@anu.edu.au
This title is also available online at: http://epress.anu.edu.au/knowledge_citation.html

---

National Library of Australia Cataloguing-in-Publication entry

Title:	Bridging the 'know-do' gap : knowledge brokering to improve child wellbeing / edited by Gabriele Bammer with Annette Michaux and Ann Sanson.
ISBN:	9781921666407 (pbk.) 9781921666414 (eBook : pdf)
Notes:	Includes bibliographical references.
Subjects:	Knowledge management--Social aspects. Communication in human services. Communication in the social sciences. Children--Services for.

Other Authors/Contributors:
        Bammer, Gabriele.
        Michaux, Annette.
        Sanson, Ann.

Dewey Number: 362.7072

Cover design and layout by ANU E Press

Cover image: ANU E Press

Contents

Setting the scene

Cases of successful knowledge brokering

Future considerations

Acknowledgments

This book is a product of the Australian Research Alliance for Children and Youth (ARACY) Research Network, which is jointly funded by the Australian Research Council (ARC) and the National Health and Medical Research Council (NHMRC). It was developed in partnership between the ARACY Research Network and two constituent organisations: The Benevolent Society and The Australian National University's National Centre for Epidemiology and Population Health. The conference organising and early chapter editing were shared between Gabriele Bammer, Annette Michaux and Ann Sanson. Most of the final editing and liaison concerning the book production was undertaken by Gabriele Bammer.

We acknowledge symposium participation and inputs from Fiona Arney, Jeremy Boland, Maree Leech and David Vicary, who were unable to contribute to the final volume. Maree Leech's contribution was based on Marie Leech, Caryn Anderson and Catherine Mahony, 'Research–practice–policy intersections in the Pathways to Prevention project: reflections on theory and experience' (in A. France and R. Homel [eds] 2007, *Pathways and Crime Prevention: Theory, policy and practice*, Willan, pp. 247–70). Fiona Arney's contribution has been published as Holzer, P., Lewig, K., Bromfield, L., & Arney, F. (2008). *Research Use in the Australian Child and Family Welfare Sector*, Australian Institute of Family Studies. http://www.aifs.gov.au/nch/pubs/reports/researchutilisation/stage1/research.pdf.

Valuable assistance in producing the book was provided by Sharyn Bant and, before her, Kelly Rae, Emma Lockwood and Carl Moller. Jan Borrie and Sharyn Bant copyedited the chapters, with Scott Stone, Jennifer Hoey and Jono Willis assisting with the figures. Duncan Beard shepherded the book through the production process and Nausica Garcia Pinar designed the cover.

Australian Research Alliance
for Children & Youth

benevolent society

ANU
THE AUSTRALIAN NATIONAL UNIVERSITY

Preface

J. Fraser Mustard

The chapter by Cathy Humphreys and Richard Vines begins with a quotation: 'As the diameter of our knowledge increases, the circumference of our ignorance expands.' The mission of the Australian Research Alliance for Children and Youth (ARACY) is to better integrate the developing knowledge about early child development and reduce ignorance in society. For ARACY, collaboration is the key to identifying and attacking the important and complex problems that have resisted solutions. They have developed this project in collaboration with their partner institutions, The Benevolent Society and the National Centre for Epidemiology and Population Health at The Australian National University.

This book, entitled *Bridging the Know–Do Gap: Knowledge brokering to improve child wellbeing*, is a good example of the effect of new knowledge expanding our understanding of human development and the effects of early development on health, learning and behaviour throughout the life cycle. The different sectors of society that are affected by this new knowledge have varying degrees of ignorance about the implications of the new knowledge.

There are a number of historical examples in the literature about the effects of new knowledge on our understanding of the human race and our societies. It took from Copernicus to Newton (more than 100 years) to overcome the belief that the Sun rotated around the Earth. The difficulty of introducing this new knowledge into Western culture was due in part to ignorance and the challenge of new knowledge to existing beliefs and religions. Another example of the translation of the new knowledge into public policy was the application of John Snow's observations about the effect of the Broad Street pump on cholera in London. In this case, there was evidence that the water supply was causing the cholera epidemic but we did not know why. Because water from the pump appeared to affect the population, the new knowledge was, however—after some controversy—accepted and applied in communities to provide clean water supplies. Only later did we learn that the bacteria in the water were causing cholera. These two examples are among many that demonstrate the effects of new knowledge on human understanding of our planet, social environment, health and wellbeing.

In the twenty-first century, we face a similar challenge of new knowledge testing our present beliefs and understanding of how early human development affects health, learning and behaviour throughout the life cycle. Until recently, we had a poor understanding of how early child development affects the architecture and function of the brain in early life and sets the neurobiological pathways that affect health, learning and behaviour throughout the life cycle.

Today we understand from work in the developmental neurobiological sciences that the architecture and function of the brain are largely set in early life (neonatal to age six) and that this stage affects the next stages of human development. We are now beginning to understand how this early period of development influences behaviour and learning, as well as the risk of coronary heart disease, high blood pressure, mental illness and many other problems. Many of the health problems will not emerge until adult life and it has been difficult for investigators to focus on how the early years of neurobiological development set pathways that affect health in later life. Our concepts of health and health care are based largely on studies of the health problems that occur in adult life, not how the risks are in fact set up in early development. This is a know–do gap.

Another example of the gap between our knowledge and what we do comes from studies of literacy. The primary belief until recently in education has been that schools and parents are crucial for the development of literacy and cognitive ability in young children. Today we know that the base for literacy development in the school system is significantly influenced by the development of the brain in the early period of human development. Despite this new knowledge, however, we still put great pressure on the school system to improve literacy rather than increasing our investment in early development.

In developed countries such as Canada and Australia, about 25 to 30 per cent of children entering compulsory education at age six demonstrate poor early development in terms of the architecture and function of the brain. The largest percentage of children showing poor early development is in the lowest socioeconomic class. About 40 per cent of the children in this class show poor early development, while 60 per cent demonstrate good development. About 12 per cent of children in the highest socioeconomic class show poor early development. Measures of early child development—when plotted against the socioeconomic background of the children—show a linear gradient. Although those in the lowest social class are the most affected by the social environment, 60 per cent of the children in the lowest social class still do well. Because of the size of the middle class, this finding demonstrates that the largest number of children with poor early development is in the middle class. Thus, although programs to improve early development for children in the lowest social class are important, targeting this population alone will miss children in the middle class and the higher socioeconomic class. These children would also benefit from making the new knowledge about early development available to all families, communities and institutions concerned with the first stage of human development. This finding has implications for public policy in the sense that all programs to improve human development should be universal. This is another example of the know–do gap.

Human development can be broken down into several stages. The first stage is from conception to age six. The second stage is from age seven to age fourteen. The third stage is from age fourteen to age twenty. The fourth stage is adult life. Each of these stages affects the next stage of development. *The Economist* magazine has recently published a series of articles about the demand in society for talent to cope with the exponential growth in new knowledge and technologies (see, for example, Wooldridge 2006). They point out that building literate, pluralistic, stable democratic societies requires that if we are to continue our experiments in civilisation, societies will have to ensure equity in early development to have a talented adult population in the future.

Today we better understand how experience-based brain development in the early years of life sets neurological and biological pathways that affect health (physical and mental), literacy and learning, and behaviour throughout the life cycle. It is important to recognise that since all the neurons in an individual's brain have the same DNA, there have to be biological pathways during early development that affect the function of the DNA in neurons. This makes it possible for neurons during early development to differentiate for their functions in vision, hearing, emotions and other neuron functions. The regulation of neuron function is influenced by epigenetics and micro-RNAs. Experience in early life affects neuron function in different parts of the brain. Identical twins have the same DNA in their neurons, but, because of these biological pathways that can alter the function of normal DNA, identical twins as adults can have a 20–30 per cent variance in behaviour. It appears that these processes, which affect normal neuron function, take place during the early period of development. In assessments of this neurobiological process, it has been demonstrated that there are qualitative differences at the different stages of development. There is something fundamentally different prenatally versus infancy versus childhood versus adulthood. We also know that higher levels of brain circuits depend on precise reliable information from lower levels in order to accomplish their function. Sensitive periods for development of lower-level circuits end early in life. The higher-level circuits remain plastic for a longer period.

This new knowledge about how stimulation in early life affects the architecture and function of the brain has ramifications for almost all academic disciplines. This new knowledge is obviously of enormous importance for the health sciences, education, economics, psychology, political science and other disciplines. One of the challenges in closing the gap between what we now know and what we do in regard to human development is that most adults working in health care, education, economics, political science, and so on, do not yet have a common base of understanding of how experience-based brain development in the early years of life affects health, learning and behaviour. It is difficult for individuals brought up in the existing institutional and disciplinary structure of our universities to introduce into their work this new knowledge about neurobiological development in the early years. We have increased demands in the healthcare sector for more money for diagnostic and treatment services, but little demand for the support of early human development to prevent health problems in adult life and enhance talented individuals in adult life. In the case of mental health problems and addiction, in Canada, the cost to individuals and society is more than $100 billion per annum. The cost in Canadian society for the effects of antisocial behaviour (crime and violence) on individuals and society is also more than $100 billion per annum. Although the evidence is robust about these costs, it is difficult to apply them to prevention and enhancing the talent of the population to improve early human development. The cost of a universal program to improve early child development in Canada for all families with young children would be about $20–22 billion per annum. The political issue around this cost equation is that the benefits from improving early human development would not be manifest until adult life. It is therefore difficult for politicians to take steps to put in place universal high-quality early human development programs in their societies. The Scandinavian countries appear to be better able to do this than English-speaking cultures.

The chapters in this book bring out the difficulties of establishing the trans-disciplinary or interdisciplinary studies that better link the results from different disciplines to provide a more integrated picture of how the social environment gets under the skin to affect the neurobiological pathways that affect the health and wellbeing of populations. The chapters are all in keeping with the role of ARACY and its partners to identify and tackle important and complex problems that have resisted solutions in most societies. Further, the chapters make the point that these key problems can be addressed by sharing strategic thinking, research design and the findings. The significance of ARACY and its partners in this is that they represent new institutions that can achieve trans-disciplinary research and improve our understanding of early development in respect to health, learning and behaviour. The success of ARACY and its partners in doing this will reduce the risk of the exponential growth in new knowledge about human development increasing the circumference of our ignorance about early human development.

References and further reading

McCain, M. N. and Mustard, J. F. 1999, *Early Years Study: Reversing the real brain drain*, Publications Ontario, Toronto.

McCain, M. N., Mustard, J. F. and Shanker, S. 2007, *Early Years Study 2: Putting science into action*, Council for Early Child Development, Toronto.

Mustard, J. F. 2008, *Early Childhood Development: The best start for all South Australians*, Adelaide Thinker in Residence, South Australian Department of Education and Children's Services, Adelaide.

Mustard, J. F. 2010, 'Early brain development and human development', in R. E. Tremblay, R. G. Barr, R. V. de Peters and M. Boivin (eds), *Encyclopedia on Early Childhood Development*, Centre of Excellence for Early Childhood Development, Montreal, Quebec, pp. 1–5, viewed 3 May 2010, <http://www.child-encyclopedia.com/documents/MustardANGxp.pdf>

Stanley, F. J., Richardson, S. and Prior, M. 2005, *Children of the Lucky Country?: How Australian society has turned its back on children and why children matter*, Pan Macmillan Australia, Sydney.

Szyf, M., McGowan, P. and Meaney, M. J. 2008, 'The social environment and the epigenome', *Environmental and Molecular Mutagenesis*, vol. 49, pp. 46–60.

Wooldridge, A. 2006, 'The battle for brainpower: a survey of talent', *The Economist*, 10 July 2006, pp. 2–24.

Introduction

Gabriele Bammer, Annette Michaux and Ann Sanson

Our children are our future. Good health and wellbeing in the early years are the foundations of well-adjusted and productive adult lives and fully functioning societies. How can we minimise disease, stop neglect and abuse and provide safe, nurturing environments? Such questions exercise the minds of members of the community at large, policymakers, the providers of various services, researchers and young people themselves. We can think of these five groups as a pentagon of stakeholders. One major challenge is to devise ways for these five groups to work in synchrony. Does synchrony matter so much? The answer is a resounding 'yes'. It seems that our efforts around the world to address the needs of children and their families are fractured and ineffective owing to our failure to learn from different sectors and integrate new knowledge.

In this book, we focus on three of the groups—policymakers, service providers and researchers—to examine how we can enhance their ability to work together. Our particular emphasis is on how we can improve the uptake of sound research evidence into government policy and into service provision. How can research knowledge be brokered to achieve effective decision making and action that improve children's wellbeing? Our aim is to provide examples of different ways this can be achieved, as well as laying foundations for further development of knowledge-brokering initiatives.

We organised a stimulating exchange between these three groups, by inviting six researchers, five service providers and three former policymakers to each write a paper based on their experience of, or interest in, successfully working across the 'know–do' gap. This was based on a method developed by one of us (Bammer and the Goolabri Group 2007). Each participant was given two of resulting papers to read and comment on, where possible, from the 'other' groups. Then, in September 2007, we brought everyone together in a one-day symposium to present and discuss these commentaries. Finally, the participants were invited to revise their papers in light of the symposium conversations. It is that collection of revised papers that we present here.

The exchange itself is the product of a unique Australian undertaking—the Australian Research Alliance for Children and Youth (ARACY)—which was established to bring together a range of organisations concerned about 'worrying trends in the wellbeing of Australia's young people' (<www.aracy.org.au>).

ARACY (through its Research Network jointly funded by the Australian Research Council and the National Health and Medical Research Council) partnered with two of its constituent organisations: The Benevolent Society and The Australian National University's National Centre for Epidemiology and Population Health. Each of these organisations has a particular interest in 'knowledge brokering' not only between research, policy and practice, but including the other corners of the pentagon: young people and the wider community.

For ARACY, the imperative has been to bring a national focus on working together in new, collaborative ways in order to find solutions to the complex problems affecting our children and young people. Using the latest information technology to overcome the 'tyranny of distance' across the nation, ARACY has become a broker of collaborations, a disseminator of ideas and an advocate for Australia's future generations.

The Benevolent Society is increasingly recognising the importance of bringing both a client/community and a practice perspective to policy and research debates, as well as trying to find better ways of integrating research into its work with children and families. It has experimented with a number of strategies to improve its contribution to the sector, including establishing knowledge-brokering roles in the organisation and investing in systems to support cross-sector learning.

At The Australian National University, one of us (GB) has suggested that improving research support for decision making and practice change should be a major pillar of the new cross-cutting discipline of Integration and Implementation Sciences (Bammer 2008). Bammer argues that improved knowledge brokering is a challenge not just for children's wellbeing, but also for many other topics in population health, education, environmental sciences and national security. There is no institutional base for allowing exchange across these areas to occur, so it is difficult for population health researchers, policymakers and practitioners, for example, to learn from the experiences of groups working on other social problems. A primary task of the new discipline is to stimulate such cross-fertilisation. Thus, while this book is designed largely for those working in the field of child wellbeing, its lessons have much broader relevance.

As our organisational summaries and the chapters in this book demonstrate, there is no one model for the activity that we abbreviate as 'knowledge brokering'. Indeed it is the diversity of possibilities that makes this a fertile and exciting area. Organisations can work together to jointly produce and implement new knowledge. Key players can work independently, but institute clear communication channels to allow them to leverage from each other.

Organisations can be established as clearing houses. Powerful individuals can advocate for the disenfranchised. The book provides examples of all of these and more.

The structure of the book

The book has three sections, beginning with setting the scene. Ann Sanson and Fiona Stanley examine the current conditions in which children and youth in Australia grow up in order to demonstrate the need for knowledge brokering. They present research on the disturbing lack of progress in improving the life chances of young people, particularly in reducing inequalities between various population groups. Sanson and Stanley then highlight instances where knowledge is available but is not being fully applied in policy or practice. This is particularly the case for evidence that developmental pathways are complex, which points to the need for policy and practice to address upstream causal determinants of child health and wellbeing, rather than responding to problems when they occur. It was strong resolve to address these issues that led to the creation of ARACY and the chapter concludes by profiling some recent ARACY initiatives aimed at advancing capacity to capture and use knowledge to improve the health, development and wellbeing of children and youth.

In the second section, six case studies of successful knowledge brokering are presented. The first three—by Annette Michaux, Robyn Cummins and Meredith Edwards, respectively—focus on knowledge brokering as engagement between the sectors. They are followed by three chapters describing different roles played by individuals who act as knowledge brokers. One (Richard Vines) works closely with a research professor (Cathy Humphreys) providing a two-way conduit for informing research of policy and practice priorities and for research implementation. Another (Sharon Goldfeld) has employment that allows her to straddle the research and policy worlds. The third is US film director Rob Reiner, whose use of his high profile to exert influence is described by Linda Neuhauser. Importantly, each of these chapters also draws attention to a different key literature about knowledge brokering. Each of these chapters is now described in more detail.

Annette Michaux leads off with a view from the non-profit practice world describing the importance of engagement and learning between sectors, as well as some of the barriers that practice organisations experience in achieving this. She highlights that a key contribution of non-profit organisations is their connection to communities and she describes a number of promising practice examples of enhanced knowledge sharing. These include the role played by cross-sectoral project teams and committees, secondments and co-locations, cross-sectoral forums and knowledge-brokering organisations. She describes The Benevolent Society's evidence-based parenting programs, as well as the organisation's involvement in 'Partnership in the Community' projects. She highlights that taking such successes to scale is now a key challenge.

Robyn Cummins describes the work of The Spastic Centre on cerebral palsy to show how it has expanded its traditional roles of knowledge brokering between researchers, practitioners and policymakers to also include consumers and the corporate sector. She describes two examples. One concerns an overhaul of operations to improve the use of research in service provision. The second involves tracking service innovation in providing intensive family support options. This was independently evaluated and the results were then used to change government funding arrangements. She also describes how The Spastic Centre has effectively used the Internet to offer people with cerebral palsy, their parents and practitioners mutual support and connection. Further, she describes how knowledge brokering with the corporate sector has led to improved equipment for people with cerebral palsy.

Meredith Edwards specifically examines engagement from the perspective of making academic research more relevant to policy. She draws on the research of Sandra Nutley to show that the extent and strength of linkages between researchers and policymakers are among the best predictors of research use. She provides an example of the effectiveness of such linkages in developing policy on long-term unemployment in the 1990s, which she oversaw as a Deputy Secretary in the Department of Prime Minister and Cabinet. In an appendix, she provides the recollections of the key academic and policy participants.

Cathy Humphreys and Richard Vines show how engagement can be enhanced when a specific role of knowledge broker is created. Cathy Humphreys was hired as the Alfred Felton Chair in Social Work to develop new and relevant research informing practice and policy and to enhance implementation of currently under-utilised knowledge. The second task, in particular, was strengthened through the employment of Richard Vines as knowledge broker. As well as describing the major projects they were involved in, they concentrate on one where the knowledge broker assisted by bringing together people from different parts of the service system—practitioners, business managers, information technology and research personnel, and government representatives—in formal and informal conversations about opportunities and constraints associated with using research-orientated information and data systems for child-centric reforms. The knowledge-brokering role aimed to nurture a social-learning environment within which research–policy–practice collaborations could emerge.

A different perspective on the knowledge broker role is provided by Sharon Goldfeld, who straddles two domains by combining part-time research/clinical and policy positions. She focuses on the skills required by knowledge brokers such as herself, including critically appraising evidence, seeing the big picture, mediation skills, along with curiosity and listening skills. She draws together insights from John Kingdon and Mark Moore to define the knowledge broker's sphere of influence, especially in seizing opportunities to create public value. She provides examples of her knowledge-brokering role in: 1) priority setting for children in the policy context; 2) helping to set up the Victorian Child and Adolescent Monitoring System; and 3) establishing the Australian Early Development Index for planning and community development.

Linda Neuhauser also describes the role of an individual knowledge broker, but in her case it is Hollywood film director Rob Reiner (of *A Few Good Men* and *When Harry Met Sally* fame). She describes how he used his celebrity, credibility and experience to support the development, testing and dissemination of a parenting education kit, which is now made available to about 500 000 new parents in the United States each year. One of his key roles was to promote engagement between the different parties. Linda also offers a useful six-stage process for knowledge brokering with a focus on participatory approaches to include consumers.

The final section of the book provides three sets of broader considerations that are pivotal for informing future research about, and the continuing development of, knowledge brokering.

Brian Head leads off this section by drawing on his experience with ARACY to highlight the different types of knowledge held by the research, policy and practice sectors, and how fragmentation of knowledge and the complexity of the issues being addressed militate against shared understandings. He argues that collaborative networks and partnering are important means to mobilise knowledge for collective action and that this is where future developments should be heading. He outlines some effective processes, as well as challenges to collaboration.

In contrast, Michael Moore provides a salutary reminder of the challenges of knowledge sharing in the political context. He draws on his experience as a politician to challenge the assumption that knowledge sharing is a desired outcome for government. On the contrary, he provides several recent Australian examples in which governments have sought to hold onto knowledge, in accord with the saying 'knowledge is power'.

Gabriele Bammer and colleagues conclude the book by arguing that considerations of research–policy interactions need to be broadened for the field to develop. In particular, knowledge brokering needs to be put into a wider context and lessons need to be drawn from different topic areas. Bridging the research–policy divide in the area of child and youth health and wellbeing could have much to learn from similar initiatives in other areas of health, as well as in the environment, education, security and so on. They also argue that more attention must be paid to evaluation of the research–policy nexus and the limitations of research as it pertains to policy. They draw on an extensive range of literature to present differences between research and policy perspectives and ways to stimulate improved interactions.

Where next?

There is a growing literature recognising the importance of bringing together research, policy and practice knowledge, as well as the knowledge of other stakeholders, such as children, parents and other community members. Given that policymakers and practitioners have the most direct influence on the environment in which young people grow up and the services available for them, the importance of integrating sound research knowledge into their decision making and actions is paramount.

This book provides a number of considerations for effective knowledge brokering between research, policy and practice, along with exciting and insightful case examples of where successful interaction has occurred. It demonstrates that effort devoted to incorporating practical knowledge into research, as well as research knowledge into practice, is worthwhile.

We want to encourage the widespread adoption of the knowledge we present here, documentation of further successes and lessons, and continued reflection on ways to improve the interaction between research, policy and practice. Our children's future and the future of our society depend on it!

References

Bammer, G. 2008, 'The case for a new discipline of Integration and Implementation Sciences', *Integration Insights*, no. 6 (May), viewed 19 May 2010, <http://i2s.anu.edu.au/sites/default/files/integration-insights/integration-insight_6.pdf>

Bammer, G. and The Goolabri Group 2007, 'Improving the management of ignorance and uncertainty. A case illustrating integration in collaboration', in A. B. Shani, S. A. Mohrman, W. A. Pasmore, B. Stymne and N. Adler (eds), *Handbook of Collaborative Management Research*, Sage, Thousand Oaks, Calif., pp. 421–37.

Setting the scene

1. Improving the wellbeing of Australian children and youth: the importance of bridging the know–do gap

Ann Sanson and Fiona Stanley

Introduction

This chapter seeks to place the need for knowledge sharing in the context of children and youth growing up in Australia today. We present evidence of the disturbing lack of progress in improving the life chances of our young people, including continuing if not accelerating socio-demographic inequalities, and describe how a determination to address these issues led to the creation of the Australian Research Alliance for Children and Youth (ARACY). We emphasise the critical importance of an evidence-based approach to policy and practice in improving children's life chances and describe some of the obstacles to the uptake of knowledge, such as the ubiquitous 'silo' mentality and rigid organisational structures. We then highlight some instances where available knowledge is not being fully applied. For example, we know that prevalent problems such as child abuse and neglect are the result of a complex set of causal factors and that we will never have the capacity to provide effective responses to all children and youth affected by them. This leads to the conclusion that we must shift the emphasis to prevention and early intervention. Yet, the majority of resources continue to be channelled into responding to the problems rather than their causes. We end by describing some of ARACY's recent initiatives, which are aimed at advancing our capacity to use knowledge to improve the health, development and wellbeing of children and youth.

Child and youth wellbeing in twenty-first-century Australia

Australia's wealth as a nation has increased markedly over the past 30 years—a period that has also seen a number of major social changes that have influenced the context in which children grow to adulthood. These changes include

- greater workforce participation by women with children (and a concomitant increase in non-parental child care)
- changes in work mobility and reductions in job security
- increased rates of divorce and single parenthood, now experienced by more than one-quarter of all children
- women having children at an older age
- an ageing population
- changes in welfare and social security policy
- the extraordinary transformations in information technology.

In themselves, these changes do not inevitably lead to negative outcomes for children. In this era of relative overall prosperity, however, we would do well to ask whether children and young people are 'having the time of their lives' or are 'struggling with life in their times' (Eckersley 2004).

Sadly, during this same period, there have been substantial increases in many major childhood disease categories and disabilities, including mental health disorders, Type 1 diabetes, obesity, behavioural problems and neurological and developmental problems such as cerebral palsy and autism. For example, the child and youth component of the National Survey of Mental Health and Wellbeing (Sawyer et al. 2001) found that one in six children aged four to twelve years had some type of mental health problem that interfered with their daily life. Trends in pre-term births are increasing, with much of low birth weight and pre-term birth arising in social adversity. The Australian Institute for Health and Welfare's 2007 report, *Young Australians: Their health and wellbeing*, noted that mental health problems and obesity have increased among young people aged fifteen to twenty-four in recent years, as have rates of sexually transmitted infections such as chlamydia and gonococcal infection. In 2004, almost one-third of young people drank alcohol at high-risk levels and about 17 per cent were current smokers. The suicide rate among young men has quadrupled, and for young women has doubled, in the past 30 years. There are similar increases in educational problems, the incidence of substance abuse and juvenile crime rates. The 2006 Census indicated that more than 12 000 children were homeless—an increase of 22 per cent from the 2001 Census (ABS 2008). Notifications and substantiations for child abuse and neglect have risen so markedly that the child protection system is under severe stress; in the past five years, child protection notifications have almost doubled; the number of children on care and protection orders increased by 32 per cent and numbers in out-of-home care increased by 35 per cent between 2002 and 2006 (see ARACY and The Allen Consulting Group 2008).

Further, there are strong socioeconomic gradients that indicate an uneven distribution of these problem outcomes. For example, recent analyses of Waves 1 and 2 of the Longitudinal Study of Australian Children (Smart et al. 2008) showed that four to five-year-old children from financially disadvantaged families were approximately twice as likely to be 'unready' for school in terms of their social, emotional, language and cognitive development compared with other children. They were also at close to twice the risk of poor progress in their first two years of school. Overall, 43 per cent of disadvantaged children contended with five or more risk factors likely to compromise their development—compared with only 14 per cent of other children.

Australia's international standing on child and youth wellbeing is not strong. ARACY's *Report Card on the Wellbeing of Young Australians* (2008) examined Australia's standing in comparison with other Organisation for Economic Cooperation and Development (OECD) countries on eight domains of child and youth wellbeing, where internationally comparable data were available. Australia was not a leader in any domain and was generally in the bottom half or third of countries with comparable data. For example, Australia ranked twentieth out of 27 countries on infant mortality, seventh out of eight on accidental injury and twenty-first out of 30 in teenage fertility. The recent UNICEF report *The Child Care Transition* (2008) indicated the dire state of childcare funding and infrastructure in Australia, finding that ours was the third-worst childcare and early learning system in the developed world. Another UNICEF report, *Child Poverty in Perspective* (2007), found that, while Australia was about average relative to other OECD countries on some indicators of material and educational wellbeing and health and safety, it was second only to Hungary in the percentage of children living in jobless households and ranked low on other measures such as family structure, child–parent interaction and peer relationships.

ARACY's report card also paints a stark picture of the wellbeing of Aboriginal and Torres Strait Islander[1] children and youth compared with Australians overall and with other OECD countries. In many domains, their indicators were as bad or worse than the lowest of the OECD countries—for example, material deprivation (ranked 29 of 31 countries), infant mortality (26/28), low birth weight (19/19), mental health problems (23/24), school achievement (29/31), sense of belonging at school (29/30) and teenage fertility (31/31). While Aboriginal people make

---

1   Referred to from now on as Aboriginal.

up 2 per cent of the total population, they make up 9 per cent of those who are homeless and 19 per cent of those in improvised housing (MacKenzie and Chamberlain 2003). They have more than twice the rate of hospitalisations for asthma and diabetes and five times the rate of child protection substantiations (AIHW 2008). Data from the Longitudinal Study of Australian Children show that the gap between Aboriginal and non-Aboriginal children's development widens markedly from infancy to four–five years of age. Despite few differences in infancy, by four–five years of age, Aboriginal children on average were lower in all aspects of development except physical development (Sanson 2005). These data point to the importance of factors in Aboriginal children's child-rearing environments in explaining the decline in wellbeing over time.

In summary, despite our relative economic prosperity, there are many areas where the situation for children and youth has failed to improve and in too many instances it is in fact deteriorating. Social inequalities remain entrenched and could be increasing.

ARACY was formed because of shared concern about these unacceptable statistics. It brings together researchers, policymakers and service providers from diverse backgrounds from across Australia to work together to improve the wellbeing of children and young people. It seeks to encourage and support a collaborative, cross-disciplinary and cross-sectoral approach to increase effectiveness in tackling the complex problems facing children and youth. Many of these are 'wicked' problems, which are not amenable to 'quick fixes'. Enhancing our capacity to use evidence effectively to guide policy and practice is thus a key ingredient to progress. This book, and the national symposium from which it is derived, forms part of ARACY's efforts to encourage evidence-based policy and practice (see Introduction).

The case for evidence-based policy and practice

Implementing evidence-based policy and practice is foundational to ARACY's vision for improving child and youth wellbeing. It is widely acknowledged that high-quality research is needed to support effective government decision making (see The British Academy 2008). For example, governments need evidence to determine what options will 'deliver the goods' and provide best 'value for money' and what policies are likely to promote innovation and achieve best outcomes for stakeholders (see Head, this volume). In relation to practice, taking an evidence-based approach—'the conscientious, explicit, judicious use of current best evidence in making decisions' (Sackett et al. 1996)—is a matter of accountability and quality. It helps to ensure that scarce taxpayer or donated dollars are spent equitably and only on interventions of demonstrable and demonstrated worth (Spring 2007).

The shared frustrations over the persistence of 'wicked' problems such as poverty, child abuse, substance abuse and Aboriginal disadvantage that drove the formation of ARACY are matched by widespread frustration at the failure of much policy and practice to reflect the evidence base. There are missed opportunities for knowledge exchange and for research-based data to play the part they should in decisions over policy and interventions (The British Academy 2008).

Stone (2002) discusses the demand-side, supply-side and socio-cultural factors that create obstacles to the uptake of knowledge. Demand-side issues include a lack of awareness of the existence or relevance of research and limited interest in and/or capacity to absorb and use research knowledge. If policymakers and practitioners do not believe that attention to research evidence will result in better policy and practice, it will not be acted upon. Landry et al. (2003) similarly identify the valuing of research knowledge as the first of the factors leading to successful knowledge translation.

Given the demands on policymakers and their high levels of mobility, it is often difficult for them to master the evidence about the complex problems facing our children and youth. Often, the research points to multiple causal influences and long-term strategies such as prevention and early intervention where the benefits might not appear for many years—well beyond a budgetary cycle or term of government. Further, the benefits are often in portfolios other than those responsible for the initial policies or interventions. For example, the long-term benefits of the Perry Preschool Program for disadvantaged children in the United States appeared in areas such as finance (because recipients of the program held better-paying jobs and hence paid more tax), the criminal justice system (with fewer convictions and incarcerations), the education system (fewer recipients needed special programs at school) and the health system (with better physical and mental health) (Schweinhart et al. 2005). More locally, installing swimming pools in remote Aboriginal communities has been shown to improve aspects of health, education and behaviour of Aboriginal children and youth over a six-year period. The costs of this intervention—the infrastructure for the pools and community engagement—were borne mainly by portfolios other than those benefiting from them (Lehmann et al. 2003). Without a cross-portfolio approach, it can be difficult for evidence to gain traction.

Further, a critical source of knowledge is the evaluation of programs, which can be threatening to both policymakers and service providers. The Australian child and youth arena is littered with unevaluated short-term 'pilot' programs. When faced with the latest in a long run of pilot programs, one remote Aboriginal community is known to have commented that they had 'a shed full of bomber jackets' from all the pilot programs that had 'flown in and flown out'. There are also continuing programs for which there is little evaluation data and, equally problematically, interventions whose funding is withdrawn despite positive evaluations. Even when programs have been shown to be effective in one context (for example, a program evaluated on suburban white Australians), we have a history of failure to deliver them effectively to disadvantaged groups. For example, evaluation has shown that traditional public health advice has failed to reduce sudden infant death syndrome (SIDS) and birth defects in Aboriginal communities (Freemantle et al. 2007; Bower et al. 2004), although participatory action research methods are now showing promising preliminary results for SIDS (Stanley, Personal communication).

Supply-side issues can apply to both researchers and practitioners. The recent UK government publication *A Vision for Science and Society* argues that engaging with policymakers ought to be a valued part of what it is to be a scientist (Department for Innovation, Universities and Skills 2008), but most Australian research environments continue to place disincentives in the way of researchers who would like to engage in collaboration with people in other sectors for the purposes of knowledge exchange. Researchers often have poor understanding of the needs of policymakers and practitioners, such as their much tighter time lines. Ineffective communication by researchers to non-academic audiences is another limiting factor (Landry et al. 2003). The technical, lengthy and cautious modes of writing often adopted by researchers are not useful for policy and practice readers, who are time poor, do not share the same technical jargon and need the implications of the research to be clearly spelled out in short documents.

Perhaps the most important factors that can mitigate against the uptake of evidence in policy and practice are socio-cultural issues. The 'disconnect' between researchers, practitioners and policymakers, and between health, education, treasury/finance, welfare and other such sectors—where each sector operates in its own 'silo', speaks a different 'language', has different constraints and operates with different time frames—is widely acknowledged, but seldom addressed. This is compounded by the contested nature of 'knowledge' and 'evidence' in the social sciences, in comparison with medicine, where the concept of evidence-based practice has been accepted for many years (Goldfeld, this volume). When considering 'wicked' problems that have a complex set of causal factors ranging from 'upstream' influences such as social disadvantage and housing, through to 'downstream' factors such as parenting and teacher–child relationships, the 'knowledge' to be brokered or exchanged is likewise complex.

Complex causal pathways: some examples of failure to act on evidence

This problem is becoming more pressing as the challenges facing society increasingly straddle the boundaries of a number of government departments and require inputs from experts in many disciplines (The British Academy 2008). The complexity of the influences on child and youth development is reflected in Bronfenbrenner's well-known bio-ecological systems theory of development (Bronfenbrenner and Morris 2006) (see Figure 1.1). At the centre is the individual child, with their own genetic and constitutionally based characteristics. The child is embedded in the micro-system, representing their immediate environments—for example, family, school, peer group—which are the 'downstream' influences on the child. The interactions among these micro-environments—for example, the nature of the connections between a child's home and school—form the meso-system and also impact on the child. The exo-system (external environmental settings, which indirectly affect the child, such as the parent's workplace) and macro-system (the larger cultural context such as economic and political systems and cultural beliefs) represent the more 'upstream' influences. Finally, the chrono-system reflects the patterning of environmental events and transitions over the course of life.

Figure 1.1 Representation of Bronfenbrenner's socio-ecological model of development with examples of factors within each system

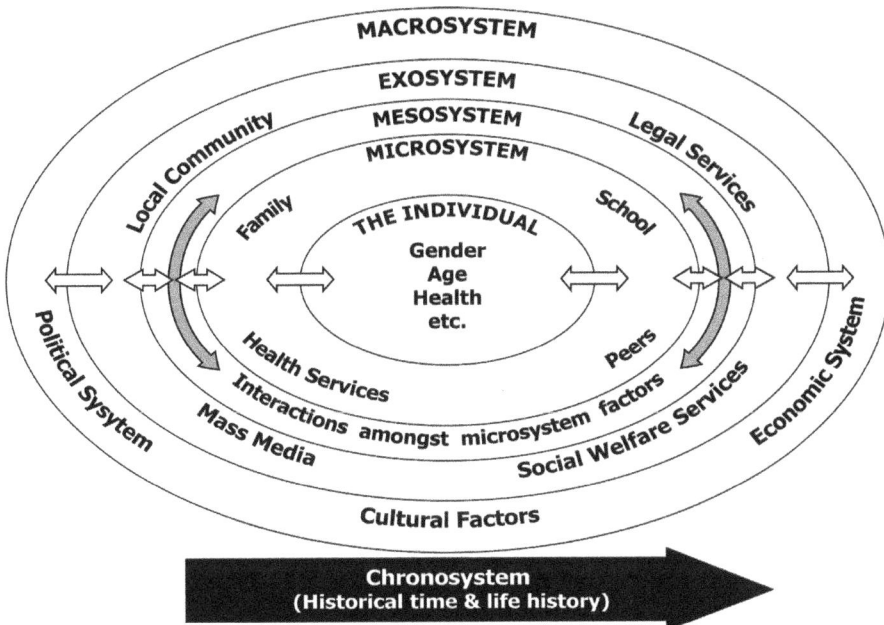

This conceptualisation of development has helped us understand 'developmental pathways' to various outcomes. Figure 1.2 is a schematic representation of the pathway to good educational outcomes, which illustrates that influences on the pathway start early in life but continue over time and are situated in each layer in Bronfenbrenner's model. Hence, there is a need for the engagement of many players in ensuring that children follow a positive pathway. If such pathways are not understood by decision makers, it can lead to attempts at 'quick fixes' addressing discrete influences at the end of developmental pathways—despite the fact that the evidence often suggests that they will be costly and relatively ineffective.

Figure 1.2 Key leverage points to improve educational outcomes

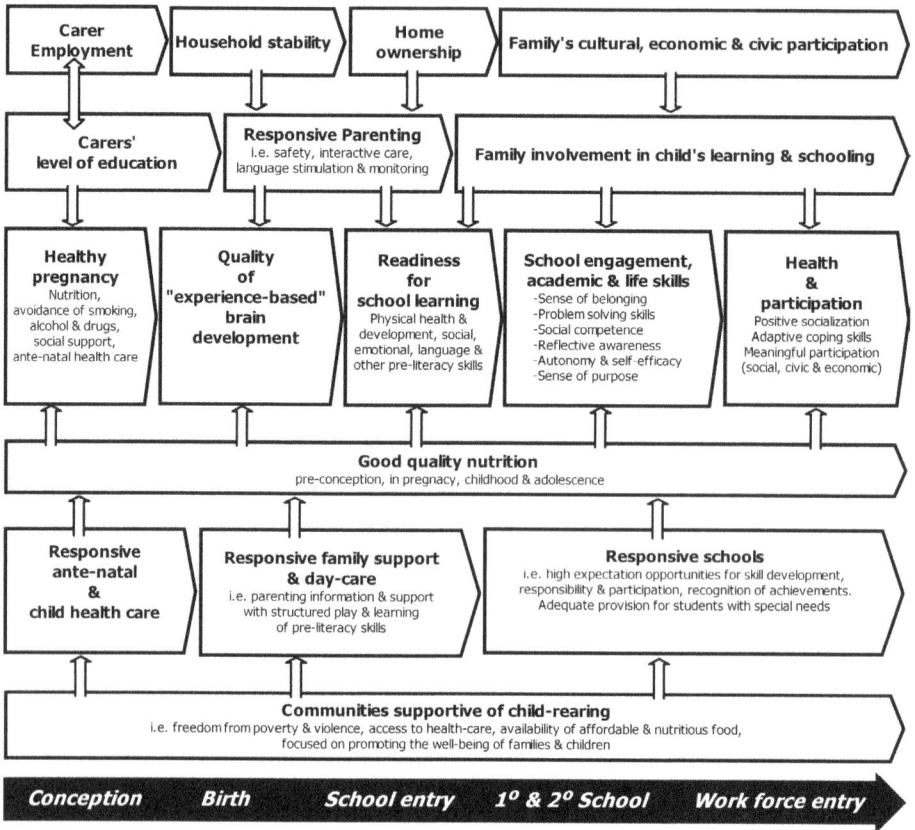

Adapted from Silburn (2009).

The current crisis in the child protection system is a good example of where we are witnessing the results of failure to address 'upstream' causal factors and where available knowledge is not being applied. Family disadvantage and instability, isolation and alienation, parental mental illness and substance abuse, lack of parenting skills as well as intergenerational factors are all known influences on the occurrence on child abuse and neglect; yet for at least a generation, the policy response to the problem of child abuse and neglect has been predominantly at the 'crisis' end, responding to allegations of abuse with measures that, intentionally or not, are punitive not only towards parents but also towards the children involved. Arguably policies have been driven too much by the imperative to save ministers from the political fallout if a child death or serious injury occurs. Services under pressure to deal with the overload of notifications do not have the resources to shift to a more preventive or supportive focus. The evidence is clear that children removed from families have far from optimal outcomes. The evidence-based alternative is to construct a multifaceted system that can provide a moderated response to all families' needs for support in order to prevent abuse and neglect in the first place, and to help those in greater need to develop their parenting abilities so that child removal becomes a rare event of last resort (O'Donnell et al. 2008). The *Wood Report* (Wood 2008:i) on the inquiry into the child protection system in New South Wales concluded that '[t]he contemporary challenge facing all child protection systems in Australia… is sufficiently resourcing flexible prevention and early intervention services so as to reduce the number of children and young people who require the state to step in to keep them safe', as well as integrated action to support those needing state intervention (see also ARACY and The Allen Consulting Group 2008). It is indeed encouraging that moves are now underway to reform the system to encompass integrated evidence-based prevention. For example, under the National Framework for Protecting Australia's Children 2009–2020 endorsed by the Council of Australian Governments (COAG), ARACY is co-convening a task force (with Minister Jenny Macklin) to develop a common approach to assessment, referral and support for vulnerable children and their families, in order to reduce the incidence of child abuse and neglect (the Common Approach to Assessment, Referral and Support (CAARS) Task Force).

The second example is what has become known as the 'Northern Territory intervention'. After years of paying scant attention to official and unofficial reports of distress and dysfunction in some Aboriginal communities, and of failure to provide adequate support for basic services such as health, policing and housing, the Federal Government 'discovered' the crisis in child abuse, neglect and ill health in 2006. An interesting analysis of how the issue came to policy prominence is provided by Moore (this volume). The response has been focused predominantly at the 'downstream' end of causal pathways, not their 'upstream' beginnings. While children's needs in the short term must obviously be addressed, long-term change requires attention to the drivers for strong family functioning, which include adequate housing and financial security, access to relevant education and meaningful occupation and their roots in community and cultural wellbeing. The intervention has paid little attention to the evidence of the importance of strong cultural continuity and community 'ownership' of initiatives that comes from research overseas, such as Chandler's work on Aboriginal youth suicide in Canada (for example, Chandler et al. 2003), and local initiatives (Zubrick et al. 2005).

ARACY's approach to overcoming the obstacles to knowledge sharing

A recurring theme in the literature on evidence-based policy and practice is the need for better dialogue, partnerships and collaboration across sectors (for example, Nutley et al. 2007). As Farfard (2008) notes, the analysis and promotion of policy options form a process of facilitating conversations and dialogue between different participants in the policy process. Key factors leading to successful knowledge translation identified by Landry et al. (2003) include the strength of not only formal links between researchers and policy makers, but informal relationships characterised by respect and trust, and collaborative working relationships. Cashmore (2003) also argues for a more collaborative process between researchers, policymakers and practitioners in order to set the research agenda, interpret findings and work out the implications for policy and practice in relation to better outcomes for children. (She also argues for including children's voices in this process, since their perceptions have an important role to play in understanding the impact of policy and practice changes.)

Evidence is accumulating about ways to facilitate these closer relationships. For example, two-way secondments between academia, government and service-provider organisations can develop understandings and connections that support knowledge transfer and provide vital insights into the needs and constraints of each sector (for further discussion, see Michaux, this volume). The notion of unidirectional knowledge exchange, whereby knowledge is generated by researchers and drawn on by policy and practice, has proven to be overly simplistic and ineffective. The advantages of a process of co-production of knowledge that aims to dissolve the boundary between evidence producers and users are also being recognised. In co-production models, all stakeholders are engaged and brought together from the outset of the research and all forms of expertise—research, policy, practice, business, the media, and so on—are considered valuable inputs into knowledge innovation, knowledge production and knowledge transfer. There is evidence that involving research users throughout the entire research process in this way increases the impact and take-up of the findings (for example, RELU 2007).

ARACY uses its status as a 'boundary organisation' (see Introduction), spanning the traditional disciplinary and sectoral silos, to develop these ideas and apply them to stimulate a more evidence-based approach to tackling the 'big-picture' issues confronting children and youth. Its report card, previously mentioned, is one undertaking aimed at bringing evidence to the fore and using it as an impetus for action. Several other examples of ARACY's knowledge-sharing initiatives follow.

The first example is ARACY's Collaboration Program, in which it is working with researchers, practitioners and experts in a range of fields related to poverty, social inclusion, early childhood development and education as well as social entrepreneurship, business and other groups who can drive ideas into action. It has developed a model for collaboration that starts by commissioning a focusing paper that draws together current evidence on a topic. This is then used as a basis for national consultations and think tanks with practitioners, stakeholders and experts from all sectors around Australia, from which an agenda and concrete proposals for action are developed and a business case is prepared to secure resources for implementation. Examples of current collaboration projects are

- *children's readiness to learn*—aiming to identify the points of intervention where most benefit will be achieved in reducing the impact of poverty on children's ability to learn
- *disengaged youth*—a cross-sectoral collaborative project aimed at preventing aggressive and violent behaviour among young people
- *measuring the outcomes of community organisations*—focusing on measures of service quality, outcomes and effectiveness, and linking these to strategies that improve support for community service organisations.

In a second example, ARACY was commissioned by the Australian Government to provide support to the 45 Communities for Children Projects in disadvantaged areas across Australia. Projects were asked to identify areas where they needed access to the best evidence (for example, how to encourage community participation; what constitutes child-friendly communities and how are they built) and researchers were asked to synthesise knowledge in these areas into accessible, short topical papers and then to discuss key practice issues emerging from the evidence with the projects. To overcome the 'tyrannies of distance', these discussions were held as 'webinars' (web seminars), whereby project members even in remote locations could interact in real time using the Internet and teleconferencing.

The third example is the Seed-Funding Program run by the ARACY ARC/NHMRC (Australian Research Council/National Health and Medical Research Council) Research Network. Recognising that time and resources are needed to develop relationships and mutual understanding between parties who have not previously worked together, this program has sought to build innovative sustainable cross-sectoral collaborations by offering seed funding on specified topic areas. These support collaborative teams to develop their project ideas to the stage where they can seek external funding. Over the four years to 2009, 51 projects have been supported, involving 542 collaborators. Evaluation has shown that the program is highly successful, leading to the development of national research agendas, sustainable cross-sectoral networks and useful resources. The program has already shown a strong return on investment in terms of successful research grants to allow projects to expand their work. The evaluation is also providing information on the factors that promote and impede successful collaborations.

Another initiative of the ARACY Research Network provides the fourth example. In order to build the capacity of the next generation of researchers to work together across disciplines and to engage in effective knowledge transfer, the Research Network has established the New Investigators Network. It currently consists of 20 high-calibre early career researchers and a team of senior mentors and advisers, who are using the Longitudinal Study of Australian Children dataset as a common base to develop collaborative projects on child and youth health and development. These young researchers are being groomed to be future research leaders who can interface with policy and practice more effectively.

Another approach to advancing our national capacity for sharing and using knowledge is to bring together those with expertise in knowledge brokering to share their experiences and then to capture them for others to learn from. Adopting this approach, the ARACY Research Network partnered with two of its member organisations to hold the national symposium on which this book is based.

References

Australian Bureau of Statistics (ABS) 2008, *Australian Census Analytic Program: Counting the homeless, Australia 2006*, cat. no. 2050.0, reissued 18 September 2008, Commonwealth of Australia, Canberra.

Australian Institute for Health and Welfare (AIHW) 2007, *Young Australians: Health and wellbeing 2007*, Australian Institute of Health and Welfare, Canberra.

Australian Institute for Health and Welfare (AIHW) 2008, *Child Protection Australia 2006–07*, Child Welfare Series no. 43, Australian Institute for Health and Welfare, Canberra, viewed 3 May 2010, <http://www.aihw.gov.au/publications/cws/cpa06-07/cpa06-07-20080229.pdf>

Australian Research Alliance for Children and Youth (ARACY) 2008, *Report Card on the Wellbeing of Young Australians*, Australian Research Alliance for Children and Youth, Canberra.

Australian Research Alliance for Children and Youth (ARACY) and The Allen Consulting Group 2008, *Inverting the Pyramid: Enhancing systems for protecting children*, The Allen Consulting Group, Melbourne.

Bower, C., Eades, S., Payne, J., D'Antoine, H. and Stanley, F. 2004, 'Trends in neural tube defects in Western Australia in Indigenous and non-Indigenous populations', *Paediatric and Perinatal Epidemiology*, vol. 18, pp. 277–80.

Bronfenbrenner, U. and Morris, P. A. 2006, 'The bioecological model of human development', in W. Damon and R. M. Lerner (eds), *Handbook of Child Psychology.Volume 1*, John Wiley & Sons, New York, pp. 793–828.

Cashmore, J. 2003, 'Children's participation in family law matters', in C. Hallett and A. Prout (eds), *Hearing the Voices of Children: Social policy for a new century*, Falmer Press, London.

Chandler, M. J., Lalonde, C., Sokol, B. and Hallett, D. 2003, *Personal persistence, identity development, and suicide: a study of native and non-native North American adolescents*, Monographs of the Society for Research in Child Development, serial no. 273, vol. 68, no. 2.

Department for Innovation, Universities and Skills 2008, *A Vision for Science and Society: A consultation for developing a new strategy for the UK*, July, Government of the United Kingdom, London, viewed 3 May 2010, <http://webarchive.nationalarchives.gov.uk/tna/+/http://www.dius.gov.uk/consultations/documents/A_Vision_for_Science_and_Society.pdf/>

Eckersley, R. 2004, *Well & Good: How we feel & why it matters*, Text Publishing, Melbourne.

Farfard, P. 2008, *Evidence and Healthy Public Policy: Insights from health and policy sciences*, May, National Collaborating Centre for Healthy Public Policy, Canada, viewed 3 May 2010, <http://www.cprn.org/documents/50036_EN.pdf>

Freemantle, J., Officer, K., McAullay, D. and Anderson, I. 2007, *Australian Indigenous Health—Within an international context*, Cooperative Research Centre for Aboriginal Health, Darwin, viewed 3 May 2010, <http://www.crcah.org.au/publications/downloads/AustIndigneousHealthReport.pdf>

Landry, R., Lamari, M. and Amara, N. 2003, 'The extent and determinants of the utilization of university research in government agencies', *Public Administration Review*, vol. 63, no. 2, pp. 192–205.

Lehmann, D., Tennant, M., Silva, D., McAullay, D., Lannigan, F., Coates, H. and Stanley, F. 2003, 'Benefits of swimming pools in two remote Aboriginal communities in Western Australia: intervention study', *British Medical Journal*, vol. 327, pp. 415–19.

Mackenzie, D. and Chamberlain, C. 2003, *Counting the Homeless 2001*, Report prepared for Commonwealth Department of Family and Community Services, Australian Bureau of Statistics, Canberra.

Nutley, S., Walter, I. and Davies, H. 2007, *Using Evidence: How research can inform public services*, Policy Press, Bristol.

O'Donnell, M., Scott, D. A. and Stanley, F. J. 2008, 'Child abuse and neglect—is it time for a public health approach?', *Australian and New Zealand Journal of Public Health*, vol. 32, no. 4, pp. 325–30.

Rural Economy and Land Use Programme (RELU) 2007, *Common Knowledge? An exploration of knowledge transfer*, June, Rural Economy and Land Use Programme, UK, viewed 3 May 2010, <http://www.relu.ac.uk/news/briefings/RELUBrief6%20Common%20Knowledge.pdf>

Sackett, D., Rosenburg, W., Gray, M., Haynes, B. and Richardson, W. 1996, 'Evidence based medicine: what it is and what it isn't', [Editorial], *British Medical Journal*, vol. 312, pp. 71–2.

Sanson, A. 2005, What can longitudinal studies tell us about supporting children's social and emotional wellbeing?, Paper presented at the Imagining Childhood: Children, culture and community Symposium, Charles Darwin University, Alice Springs, September.

Santrock, J. W. 2007, *Child Development*, Eleventh edition, McGraw-Hill Companies, New York.

Sawyer, M. G., Arney, F. M., Baghurst, P. A., Clark, J. J., Graetz, B. W. Kosky, R. J., Nurcombe, B., Patton, G. C., Prior, M. R., Raphael, B., Rey, J. M., Whaites, L. C. and Zubrick, S. R. 2001, 'The mental health of young people in Australia: key findings from the child and adolescent component of the national survey of mental health and well-being', *Australian and New Zealand Journal of Psychiatry*, vol. 35, no. 6, pp. 806–14.

Schweinhart, L. J., Montie, J., Xiang, Z., Barnett, W. S., Belfield, C. R. and Nores, M. 2005, *Lifetime effects: the HighScope Perry preschool study through age 40*, Monographs of the HighScope Educational Research Foundation, no. 14, HighScope Press, Ypsilanti, Mich.

Silburn, S. R. 2009, Paper presented at the National Summit—Resilience for Children (0–13 years), Parliament House, Canberra, 16 June 2009.

Smart, D., Sanson, A., Baxter, J., Edwards, B. and Hayes, A. 2008, *Home-to-School Transitions for Financially Disadvantaged Children*, The Smith Family, Sydney.

Spring, B. 2007, 'Evidence-based practice in clinical psychology: what it is, why it matters, what you need to know', *Journal of Clinical Psychology*, vol. 63, no. 7, pp. 611–31.

Stone, D. 2002, Getting research into policy, Paper presented at Global Development National Conference, Rio de Janeiro, 7–10 December.

The British Academy 2008, *Punching our Weight: The humanities and social sciences in public policy making, a British Academy report*, The British Academy, London, viewed 3 May 2010, <https://www.britac.ac.uk/policy/punching-our-weight.cfm>

United Nations Children's Fund (UNICEF) 2007, *Child Poverty in Perspective: An overview of child well-being in rich countries*, Innocenti Report Card 7, UNICEF Innocenti Research Centre, Florence.

United Nations Children's Fund (UNICEF) 2008, *The Child Care Transition*, Innocenti Report Card 8, UNICEF Innocenti Research Centre, Florence.

Wood, J. 2008, *Report of the Special Commission of Inquiry into Child Protection Services in NSW*, Government of New South Wales through the Special Commission of Inquiry into Child Protection Services in New South Wales, Sydney, viewed 3 May 2010, <http://www.dpc.nsw.gov.au/publications/news/stories/special_commission_of_inquiry_into_child_protection_services_in_new_south_wales>

Zubrick, S. R., Silburn, S. R., Lawrence, D. M., Mitrou, F. G., Dalby, R. B., Blair, E. M., Griffin, J., Milroy, H., De Maio, J. A., Cox, A. and Li, J. 2005, *The Western Australian Aboriginal Child Health Survey: The social and emotional wellbeing of Aboriginal children and young people. Volume 2*, Curtin University of Technology and Telethon Institute for Child Health Research, Perth, viewed 3 May 2010, <http://www.ichr.uwa.edu.au/waachs/publications/volume_two>

Cases of successful knowledge brokering

2. Integrating knowledge in service delivery-land: a view from The Benevolent Society

Annette Michaux

People continually expand their capacity to create the results they truly desire, where new and expansive patterns of thinking are nurtured, where collective aspiration is set free, and where people are continually learning how to learn together. (Senge 1990)

Chapter aims

This chapter offers a practice perspective on three main themes. The first is the importance of learning collaborations and partnerships that move beyond access to knowledge to engagement with and use of learning, and some of the barriers that non-profit practice organisations experience in these interactions. Second, the chapter examines the contribution of non-profit organisations to policy and research due to their connection to communities; and third, the chapter outlines examples of initiatives that illustrate strategies facilitating the mediation of knowledge across sectoral and organisational boundaries.

About The Benevolent Society

At nearly 200 years old, The Benevolent Society is Australia's oldest non-profit organisation. It is a diverse organisation delivering services to people and communities, with a focus on children and families, older people and women's health. We also run leadership programs bringing people together from business, the community and government for social change. In 2009, services were provided to about 17 500 people, and we have approximately 850 staff, 600 volunteers and 350 alumni of our leadership programs. The children's services span out-of-home care, child protection, early intervention, post-adoption resources, long day care and playgroups as well as community development. More information about the organisation can be found at <www.bensoc.org.au>

Importance of knowledge integration

The Benevolent Society's purpose is to *create caring and inclusive communities and a just society*. To do this, we are rethinking how to work and moving the organisation beyond traditional service provision to a stronger focus on linking our work in communities to research and evaluation, as well as policy action (see Figure 2.1).

Figure 2.1 Linking The Benevolent Society's programs and services with research and evaluation as well as policy action

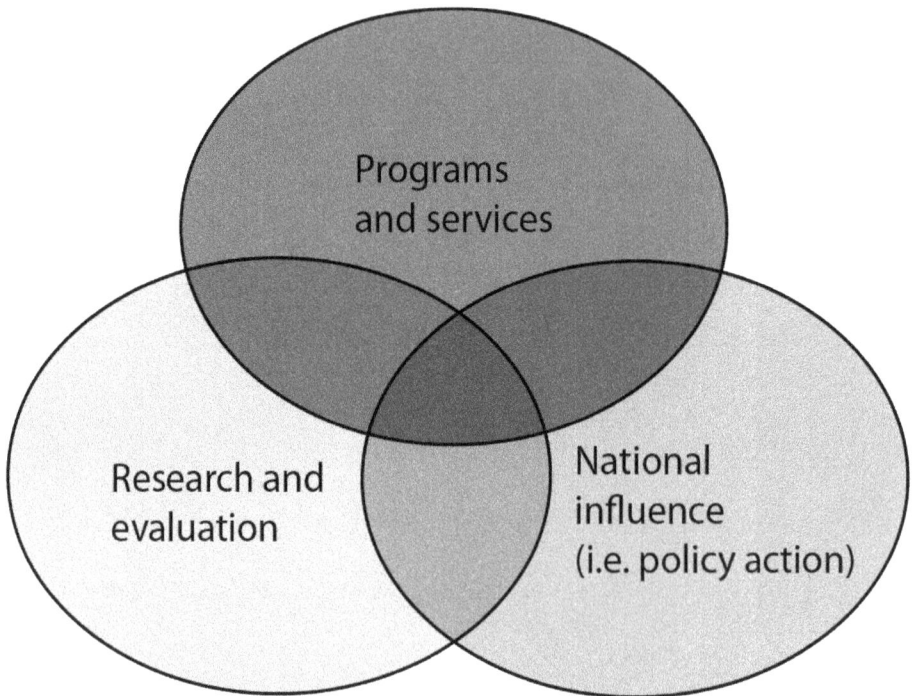

Our purpose calls for us to engage more systematically with researchers and policymakers across all levels of our organisation. Although non-profit organisations are excluded from many policy and research debates, the onus is also on non-profits to make sure we are at the table and that we present well-evaluated and constructive service models and policy ideas for the consideration of policymakers.

Increasingly, non-profit organisations are the recipients of large government contracts for service delivery. This is a positive trend, but programs can encounter difficulties when service providers are excluded from the design of programs. Non-profit organisations must be consulted during the design stage of programs, especially when international evidence is being applied to the Australian context.

Community organisations are at the heart of democratic life and civic engagement and are the only institutions with the flexibility and connections to put the policy solutions into practice on the ground.

Attempting to rise to these challenges, non-profit organisations large and small are changing their structures and investing in skills that allow them to play a leadership role at the policy and research table. For example, The Benevolent Society is investing in a comprehensive research and advocacy agenda allowing us to be judicious and strategic in the way we mediate knowledge across internal and external boundaries.

Difficulties of sharing knowledge across sectors

We find that knowledge is *sticky* and does not move easily between sectors (Szulanski 1996). In a case study of eight US firms undertaken in the 1990s, it was found that this *stickiness* was not just about motivation to learn or the greatest barrier to learning across organisations; instead it was found that organisational units did not know *how* to learn. This important insight forces us to consider learning strategies that will work in the Australian context. We know that the keys to integrating knowledge are people, relationships and interaction combined with strong learning systems, an inter-sectoral culture and good tools to facilitate learning. This requires a shift in our approach to knowledge on a number of levels and is illustrated in Figure 2.2, which I have adapted from Bill Ford's work in Australia on learning organisations.

Ford's work challenges us to look at organisations and how they work both internally and externally. The left side of Figure 2.2 shows how organisations and sectors have traditionally worked. For example, in medicine, a very distinct knowledge hierarchy can exist with medical doctors at the top and patients seen as passive recipients of treatment, rather than partners sharing information about a health problem. The middle of Figure 2.2 forces institutions to radically rethink how they structure their internal operations and relate to external networks if knowledge is to be integrated. The organisational development literature talks of flat structures with *fuzzy* boundaries where teamwork and collaboration win over traditional hierarchical models of leadership. Crutchfield and McLeod Grant (2008), in a study of successful non-profit organisations in the United States, emphasise that collaborative models are more effective than others in forging policy change. The non-profit organisations that have policy impact tend to excel at influencing players outside their boundaries, managing complex networks and relationships through partnerships and coalitions. These organisations tend to have distributed leadership throughout their organisation ensuring that there is high-level engagement with learning how to overcome the social issue at hand.

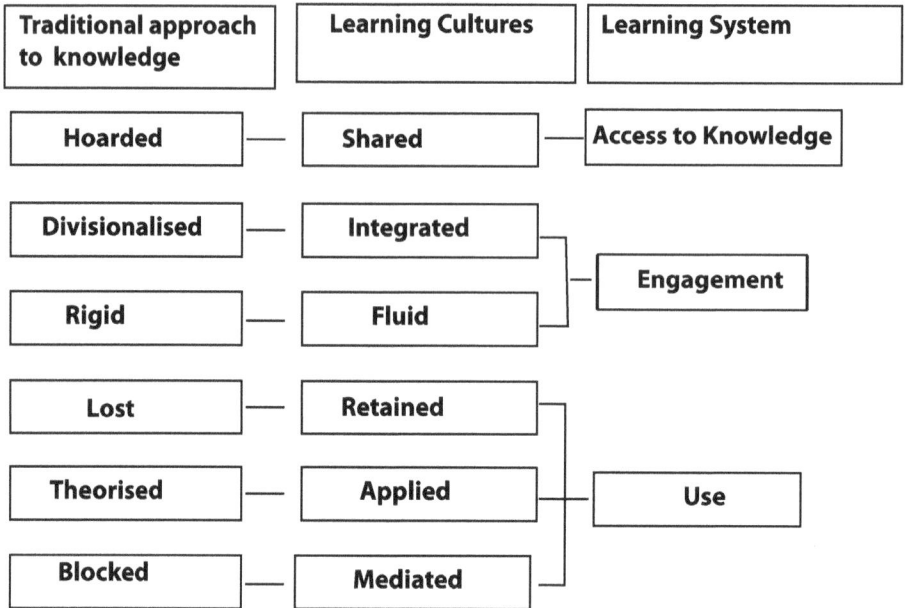

Traditional approach to knowledge	Learning Cultures	Learning System
Hoarded	Shared	Access to Knowledge
Divisionalised	Integrated	
Rigid	Fluid	Engagement
Lost	Retained	
Theorised	Applied	Use
Blocked	Mediated	

Figure 2.2 Elements involved in moving from traditional approaches to knowledge to learning cultures and learning systems

Adapted from Bill Ford (1999).

The other area of interest to us is the different cultures that arise in different professional groups, as well as the inter-professional hierarchies, with some professions more highly regarded than others. For example, we have observed that early childhood professionals—in particular, those involved in the childcare sector—are often shut out of policy debates about children, reflecting perceptions about their status.

To support knowledge flow across these boundaries, we need to find new, integrated and sustainable systems for bringing people together to learn (the right side of Figure 2.2). The view from service delivery-land is that we have some excellent *access* to knowledge through a variety of Australian clearing houses and their disseminated publications. We struggle, however, to find ways to ensure there is *engagement* with this knowledge and therefore its translation into *use*. Later in this chapter, I draw on some examples of how we have moved beyond *access* at The Benevolent Society.

Why partnerships are important: the contributions of non-profit organisations to policy and research

Too often those closest to a policy issue or research question are excluded from decision-making processes. Clients and communities on the receiving end of policy as well as the non-profit organisations that are best positioned to respond are not at the table. In Australia, while there is increasing talk of whole-of-government responses, there is no corresponding attention to whole-of-sector responses. Until recently, non-profit organisations were discouraged from advocacy work for social change and sometimes punished and silenced for engaging in policy debates (Hamilton 2007).

The literature on organisational development and partnerships as well as the drive for *joint* work in the United Kingdom (Ford 1999; Mandell 2006; Anning et al. 2006) show that, to implement what works for children, we have to find new ways of working and learning that are supported by very different institutional arrangements. The community sector could hold the key to some of the more creative and flexible arrangements needed to facilitate this major change and must therefore have a greater voice.

Non-profit organisations play an important role in generating research questions and identifying research gaps. We also have the flexibility to be innovative and responsive and to test new ideas. A growing number of philanthropists who are interested in social change organisations such as The Benevolent Society can organise financial backing for research and learning opportunities that might be considered too risky for government. A recent Australian example of this is the work of the philanthropist Chris Cuffe, who is using innovative approaches to fundraising to generate a steady income stream for the organisation Social Ventures Australia, of which The Benevolent Society and The Smith Family are founding partners (Horin 2008).

Despite the relatively slow start in Australia to engaging philanthropy, it is now poised to play a key role in funding innovation and research and as an additional partner in knowledge integration. Although not the focus of this chapter, this is an exciting development being explored.[1]

---

1 See, for example, the role of philanthropy in the Pathways to Prevention Project (Homel et al. 2006).

We are keen to see knowledge *flow* from practice to research as well as from research to practice. We believe that non-profit organisations can play a significant role as knowledge producers. Framing research questions based on our practice wisdom often generates important insights into the needs of communities and thus informs policy. Our experience in developing a model for working in kinship care has revealed that there is very little Australian research to guide us. We have generated a number of research/policy questions, such as how to measure the outcomes of kinship care work and about good practice models for Indigenous families. We are now working alongside academics and government officials to develop our research agenda together.

Donald Schon's (1983) work is useful as it reveals how professionals know more than they can put into words. His work focuses on how we need to tap into this reflection-in-action and how this vital creativity (or tacit knowledge) might be fostered by organisations.

Schon argues that the best planners, architects, engineers and psychologists cannot always say what they know how to do, but reflective processes are a way of harnessing and sharing this greater problem-solving ability. Good organisations find ways to allow a broader context for reflective inquiry and count it as a legitimate form of professional knowing (Schon 1983).

This process is not easy. The knowledge we hold in community services is often complex, hard to teach and hard to detach from the person who created it. Think of the incredibly complex interactions and processes involved in the way a very good practitioner goes about their work with a family, and in their interactions with that family's community. As Smith (2001) states, this sort of complex know-how cannot just be transmitted; 'it has to be engaged with, talked about and embedded in organisational structures and strategies'. We have found that supervision sessions alongside group learning opportunities such as communities of practice and learning circles open up the creative space for people to engage and share this tacit knowledge. Bringing a wider network to the table during these knowledge-production sessions is an important way for research and policy to connect with communities (see the section on inter-agency learning forums in this chapter).

Non-profit organisations such as The Benevolent Society have a strong connection to people in their communities and are often in a position to consider community needs as well as strategies for effectively translating research into practice. We are a rich source of case studies and evaluative data about child and family practice. We can also play the role of reminding researchers and policymakers to treat people as participants and partners in processes rather than as objects of concern to 'do things to'. Service delivery organisations such as The Benevolent

Society are well placed to ensure that research and evaluation in communities can be empowering, enabling processes for participants in which the journey of knowledge generation is as significant as the destination.

Our limitations in the conversation

There is often a gap in the conversation between research, policy and practice. This has been described as the product of their different cultures (Shonkoff 2000; Tsui 2006). Speaking different languages makes communication between sectors difficult. Practitioners can find it hard to articulate research questions and we are sometimes inarticulate about our work and the nature and extent of a problem in a community. We can also lack policy and research literacy and think narrowly about problems, not seeing connections to root causes or larger social issues.

Strategies to facilitate knowledge integration: sector level

Cross-sectoral project teams, boards and committees

A well-established mechanism for collaboration includes advisory bodies, inter-sectoral committees and board appointments that ensure cross-sectoral inclusion. The make-up of these bodies should be reflected at different levels of organisations, from the most senior to local implementation levels. The committee layers of the Australian Government's Communities for Children Program are a good example of national to local inter-sectoral attempts at integration. Many project teams and working committees are considering new ways to meet and interact to reflect Australia's need for geographic inclusion including the use of telephone link-ups and moving meeting venues around the country. The Australian Research Alliance for Children and Youth (ARACY) as well as rural health and educational institutions have worked out good systems for such interactions.

Secondments and co-locations

Secondments where academics, policymakers and practitioners are *embedded* in other organisations are powerful ways to create understanding, integration and more insightful leadership. The Benevolent Society has an arrangement with the NSW Department of Community Services through which staff from each organisation spend a week swapping roles. Feedback tells us that this creates understanding and empathy between practitioners. These secondments and direct swaps have been known to take place between senior bureaucrats and academics. The Brotherhood of St Laurence, a service provider in Victoria, has several academics working between the university and the agency over the long term.

Co-locating staff from different agencies can also bring benefits (Department for Education and Skills 2003); however, our experience is that this needs to be carefully designed and that co-location alone does not produce integration, as communication problems can persist (Anning et al. 2006). Teams must be actively encouraged to work more closely. We have found that project-based work can facilitate this. Sometimes community members find that co-location does not work for them. For example, locating child protection services in schools can be highly stigmatising for parents required to visit the onsite 'welfare'.

Cross-sectoral forums

Workshops and symposia that bring policymakers and researchers together would be richer if they more regularly included and facilitated insights from skilled practitioners and community members. While this requires some planning and additional support, our experience is that the views of practitioners and community members sometimes need to be sought in more creative ways than happens in traditional modes of inquiry. We have used interview techniques to gain practitioner insights and creative tools such as artworks to understand children's reflections on a particular topic or social issue. Less formal opportunities to meet and talk also include using community festivals and exhibition-style booths where people can approach one another without feeling they are having public conversations.

Knowledge-brokering organisations

The ARACY and the Sax Institute (a NSW-based organisation that develops research products and builds partnerships between researchers and health policy and service delivery agencies for better health) are dedicated to bringing together practice, policy and research for better outcomes. Our experience of both entities is that they are facilitating new opportunities for non-profit organisations such as The Benevolent Society to be more closely involved in policy debates. This has taken the form of being invited to speak at various forums, as well as introductions to new networks and individuals, especially in the policy domain, which can be difficult for outsiders to access.

Boundary-breaking activities

Service delivery organisations that play a role in undertaking research or in policy development help break down barriers and ensure that new and more grounded perspectives are included in decision-making processes. Increasingly, the large non-profit organisations have their own research and policy analysis capacity. In New South Wales—following the lead of Victorian community organisations—we are regularly meeting to develop research themes and ideas across community agencies. For example, The Benevolent Society initiated a non-government research forum in New South Wales. In addition, the University of Sydney's Faculty of Education and Social Work has played an important role in exchanging knowledge with community services.

Knowledge-integration techniques: practice perspectives

Research shows that face-to-face contact is the best way to get evidence into the hands of those who need it (Reardon et al. 2007). We have certainly found this to be the case. Some research centres offer great promise in their responsiveness to our questions about messages from research. The following examples show some useful strategies for linking practice to research and policy.

The Benevolent Society's evidence-based parenting programs

This project aims to implement evidence-based parenting programs across our children's services. It has involved a number of challenging steps and forced us to engage with, and make decisions about, evidence and then implement a new way of working across a large and geographically diverse organisation. We have learnt that a staged approach to practice change is required—that is, one that takes account of *access*, *engagement* and *use* of knowledge. This example highlights the interaction of good people and good processes, as well as systems to implement evidence in the world of practice.

Our first and most important step in 2003 was for the management team to commit to implementing evidence-informed practice across our child and family services. This has involved some major change-management challenges. The next step was accessing the research, in order to understand and engage with it. We approached the Parenting Research Centre from Victoria to run workshops for our services on evidence-based parenting skills programs. This centre's links to practice enabled them to successfully bridge the research-to-practice divide as they spoke the same clinical language as our practitioners and helped us develop our practice in a way that made sense.

Another key ingredient was the knowledge-brokering role of one senior manager, who used a Churchill Fellowship to study parenting programs overseas. His knowledge and commitment meant we had a strong internal champion for the implementation process. This manager has been in a position to seek advice from international experts on the program and consider its application to rural and remote Australia including Indigenous families.

The next step was systematic implementation of the Incredible Years parenting program. Organisational processes needed to be shifted to foster a culture of performance around evidence-informed practice (Letts et al. 1999). This included building outcomes around the implementation into business plans, recruitment of managers with knowledge-brokering skills and improving performance-appraisal systems. We are also developing practice guidelines and making explicit the roles of managers in implementing evidence-informed practice.

This experience has helped us better understand our role in knowledge brokering. It confirms the need for designated internal staff to carry a project forward as well as strong links with the external research and practice community internationally. We have found that in practice-land we need to *engage* tenaciously with new knowledge if it is to get a foothold in *use* and practice change.

Using seminars as a springboard to practice change

Another example is a seminar on best practice in child and family work presented by the Centre for Community Child Health. The seminar was held at The Benevolent Society and we found that when we had a critical mass of managers and practitioners in the room to engage in a dialogue, we started to see practice shifts taking place as a result. This could be for several reasons, including enough people hearing the same, very well-presented message, which means they can follow it through more easily as enough people *get it*, *talk about it* and *use it*.

Inter-agency learning forums

Sometimes face-to-face contact is not possible. The Central Coast Networks of Practice (funded by Families New South Wales) offers a research-to-practice clearing house and themed practitioner newsletters. These are important regional avenues for translating research into practice, as well as for the sharing of practice wisdom. These practice networks also enable conversations between practitioners from different disciplines. The network takes the work of a number of Australian clearing houses and tailors it to the Central Coast audience. This has been a very effective way of increasing *access* to research.

Linked to Networks of Practice, but more localised, is the 2261 Services Networking Project (funded through the Commonwealth Government's Communities for Children initiative). The larger Communities for Children advisory committee was devoting little time in meetings to focusing on knowledge sharing. Although managers were able to attend some of the 'webinars' and read topical papers (knowledge-sharing tools offered through ARACY), local practitioners were not accessing these resources. A more responsive local effort was needed. The 2261 Project meets and discusses topics such as behaviour management and transition to school when there are specific practice questions. The group then discusses the issues, shares ideas and brings in speakers. The emphasis is on working through issues in a timely fashion and through informal sharing.

We have been running a strengths-based practice project (in partnership with Gowrie, Sydney, another children's service provider, funded by Families New South Wales) with a reach of 450 early childhood services. Designed by staff with excellent knowledge-brokering skills and strong links to research, the project includes broad-based dissemination as well as an intensive component working with up to 45 practitioners. Evidence on early childhood development is translated into formats and tools that early childhood workers can understand, which allows the group of 45 to engage in learning circles and other reflective learning spaces to discuss implementing new practices.

The evaluation findings show that the combination of creating accessible material and learning spaces is a powerful way of integrating knowledge. Two focus group participants reflected on their experiences as follows:

> It was the most beneficial training for Children's Service managers which I have done in 25 years as a director of a service. I wish that all new directors could be offered up to 12 months of facilitated SBP learning circles. It would save them many years of learning through trial and error.

> I was rather sceptical in the beginning and not sure that I would have the time to commit to the project but I am so glad I did as it has given me the tools and skills to approach work with staff, families and children with some validation.

Partnerships in community projects

Initiatives such as the Australian Government's Communities for Children initiative provide excellent opportunities for cross-sectoral and cross-discipline engagement through a range of local projects. They bring to life the complexities and rewards of deep engagement in community settings. They involve partnerships between community organisations, community members, social policy researchers (in this case, the University of NSW Social Policy Research Centre), local evaluators (on-the-ground researchers) and state and Commonwealth officers, with connections to organisations such as ARACY and the Australian Institute of Family Studies. Our particular Communities for Children projects (located in south-western Sydney and the NSW Central Coast) have used a local collaborative structure to take up the challenge of designing community initiatives that are evidence based and responsive to local need.

Attempts at true collaborations—that is, those efforts in which participants come together to solve a complex issue and are interdependent—are resource intensive and require strong leadership. This involves people entering into new ways of thinking, working and making changes to existing systems and structures (Mandell 2006). For example, the engagement process for the Communities for Children projects was time consuming (about 18 months of planning when the original time line was six months) and required highly skilled managers. This highlights that bringing a Commonwealth strategy to life on the ground with the added central ingredient of community participation often involves hidden and unacknowledged street-level knowledge brokering. Policy initiatives that require this level of cross-sectoral and community involvement can have unrealistic expectations and be conceptually undercooked. The evaluative work on these programs will help us better understand how to successfully negotiate such partnerships.

Partnerships in research

We have had several experiences partnering across policy, practice and research through Australian Research Council (ARC) Linkage grants. These grants can facilitate knowledge integration in the following ways

- Increased respect and the breaking down of stereotypes, as the process of deep involvement in a research project allows collaborators to understand the strengths that they and others bring, as well as appreciating the constraints that others are working under.

- Promoting understanding of organisational context. For example, in our experience, bureaucracies change over the course of the project in a way that other partners do not. Staff turnover is high and decisions must go through hierarchical processes. We have learnt to expect high turnover of personnel and the need for excellent documentation around roles, responsibilities and sign-off for the project, so that it does not drift from the original aims.

- Gaining buy-in for dissemination and implementation of research findings from partners (this is why it is important to have policy officials as partners in the projects). A project being undertaken with Queensland and Sydney universities, the Queensland Government Treasury and Mission Australia ensured that senior bureaucrats were involved in initially framing the research questions to try to ensure relevance to policy.

- Allowing 'younger' and 'older' generations to work together. Older members of the team bring wisdom and experience and younger members bring fresh ideas. Connecting young researchers and policy officers is also paving the way for long-term inter-sectoral and cross-disciplinary work in the next generation.

- Involving practitioners from the partner organisation in the research, enabling them to learn valuable skills and competencies. This involvement has led to the partner organisations having greater ownership of the results.

- Having the right people at the table to comment and correct, so that documents about the research results can be designed more effectively and timed to meet the needs of the different sectors.

- Seeking research–practice linkage projects, such as those funded by the ARC, to offer opportunities for boundary-breaking roles in non-research organisations. As a practice organisation, we have been able to employ early career researchers, as linkage projects allow for publication, presentation and student supervision opportunities alongside a deeper connection to research application. Collaborations tend to seep to other sections of organisations keen to communicate research findings. Staff members in other parts of partner organisations, such as media and public relations officers, have also enjoyed the benefits of working jointly (with researchers) on media releases and other communication strategies.

Summary of challenges and concluding thoughts

The examples in this chapter show a number of promising initiatives for better integrating knowledge. They also point to some of the many challenges.

Australia has developed some excellent knowledge-dissemination mechanisms, especially our clearing houses (for example, the four Australian Institute of Family Studies clearing houses—on different topics—and the Domestic and Family Violence Clearing House). As trusted sources of evidence, clearing houses create a firm base to build from. Australia is, however, behind many other Western nations in taking the next step to integrated cross-sectoral processes and structures to allow people to engage with and therefore use this knowledge. This is particularly challenging in a country of this size. We estimate that Benevolent Society practitioners have about five minutes a day of reading time. It is therefore unlikely that they will be able to engage with the written evidence unless we find the right systems and new ways to resource the mediation of it.

The differing time scales needed for research continue to hamper evidence-informed policy and practice. The need for rapid answers to practice and policy questions is often out of step with the nature of research grant funding and the operation of academic institutions, meaning that it is often hard to be responsive in this environment (for example, ARC Linkage grant funding processes are slow). Research and evaluation consultants can be brought in to fill this gap and we need to find ways to ensure these private providers contribute to knowledge integration.

Another constraint is the lack of recognition that academic institutions give for the kind of policy and practice research publications and activities (plain English and brief) that are useful to the field. We understand that academics face significant constraints to being involved in many of the sorts of projects that we would find useful. Academics find their important work with practitioners goes unrecognised unless it can be made into a journal article.

Collaboration in developing and undertaking the research is the first step in a process that needs to extend to implementing the findings through the policy process. There is often pressure for academics to cease their involvement when the research is complete. We need to find ways to fund follow-up activity to look at how to get research knowledge into the policy process.

Unlike researchers based in universities, the policy and practice workforce tends to be more transient, moving across agencies, departments and roles. This mobility presents constant challenges to collaborative efforts and can seriously undermine longer-term projects when a project champion moves on.

Perhaps the biggest hurdle remains the policy community's struggle to find effective ways to engage community members and community organisations. Until we engage with those at the receiving end of policy implementation, we will miss vital information about what works in Australia.

Despite the challenges outlined, I have illustrated a number of promising examples of knowledge integration. At the policy level, the new focus on social inclusion in Australia is a welcome sign that cross-sectoral efforts will guide our approach to complex social and economic issues.

We are keen to know if collaborative efforts and initiatives are making a tangible difference to children and their families. Mapping a path between knowledge brokering and better policies and practices is not easy, but it is very important that we evaluate the extent to which these efforts are achieving results.

The organisational development and knowledge integration literature (Bammer et al., this volume) points to the need for new institutional arrangements that allow for integrated learning between research, policy and practice, as well as real changes to how we roll out policies and deliver services to children and their communities. If knowledge is sticky, hoarded and theorised, it is our job as a large service provider to play a leadership role in making it runny, accessible and useable. The examples used in this chapter show it can be done. Now is the time to take our efforts to scale!

References

Anning, A., Cottrell, D., Frost, N., Green, J. and Robinson, M. 2006, *Developing Multiprofessional Teamwork for Integrated Children's Services*, Open University Press, Australia.

Crutchfield, L. and McLeod Grant, H. 2008, *Forces for Good. The six practices of high-impact nonprofits*, Jossey-Bass, San Francisco.

Department for Education and Skills 2003, *Every Child Matters*, Government of the United Kingdom, London.

Ford, B. 1998, 'Mediating knowledge', *HR Monthly*, September.

Ford, B. 1999, Diagrams on learning organisations, Unpublished ms.

Hamilton, C. 2007, *Silencing Dissent*, Allen & Unwin, Sydney.

Homel, R., Freiberg, K., Lamb, C., Leech, M., Carr, A., Hampshire, A., Hay, I., Elias, G., Manning, M., Teague, R. and Batchelor, S. 2006, *The Pathways to Prevention Project: The first five years, 1999–2004*, Mission Australia and Key Centre for Ethics, Law, Justice and Governance, Griffith University, Brisbane.

Horin, A. 2008, 'The $33m man is back—but now he's working for free', *Sydney Morning Herald*, 21 July 2008.

Letts, C. W., Ryan, W. P. and Grossman, A. 1999, *High Performance Nonprofit Organisations. Managing upstream for greater impact*, John Wiley & Sons, USA.

Mandell, M. 2006, Do networks matter: the ideals and realities, Keynote address to Government and Communities in Partnership Conference, Centre for Public Policy, University of Melbourne, 25–27 September 2006, viewed 5 May 2010, <http://www.public-policy.unimelb.edu.au/conference06/>

Michaux, A. 2006, *Learning Organisations and Why They Are Important in Community Services*, The Benevolent Society, Paddington, NSW, viewed 5 May 2010, <www.bensoc.org.au>

Reardon, R., Lavis, J. and Gibson, J. 2007, 'From research to practice: a knowledge transfer planning guide', *Insight and Action*, issue 1 (March), Canadian Health Services Research Foundation, Ottawa.

Saunders, P. and Walter, J. 2005, *Ideas and Influence. Social science and public policy in Australia*, UNSW Press, Sydney.

Schon, D. 1983, *The Reflective Practitioner: How professionals think in action*, Basic Books, New York.

Senge, P. 1990, *The Fifth Discipline. The art and practice of the learning organization*, Random House Australia, Sydney.

Shonkoff, J. P. 2000, 'Science, policy and practice: three cultures in search of a shared mission', *Child Development*, vol. 71, no. 1, pp. 181–7.

Smith, M. 2001, 'Chris Argyris: theories in action, double loop learning and organisational learning', *The Encyclopedia of Informal Education*, viewed 5 May 2010, <www.infed.org/thinkers/argyris.htm>

Szulanski, G. 1996, 'Exploring internal stickiness: impediments to the transfer of best practice within the firm', *Strategic Management Journal*, vol. 17.

Tsui, L. 2006, *A Handbook on Knowledge Sharing: Strategies and recommendations for researchers, policymakers, and service providers*, Community University Partnership for the Study of Children, Youth and Families, Alberta.

3. Building knowledge futures for cerebral palsy: examples from The Spastic Centre

Robyn Cummins

Introduction

The knowledge-brokering field has traditionally involved a triad of stakeholders: researchers, practitioners and policymakers. The Spastic Centre has a record of successful knowledge sharing and brokering in these realms, but is increasingly aware of two additional stakeholder groups with a growing influence in the field: consumers and the corporate sector. The Spastic Centre is an organisation attuned to the benefits of knowledge brokering and is now engaged in activities involving all five of these groups.

Background

Cerebral palsy is a permanent physical condition that affects movement. There are approximately 11 000 people in New South Wales with cerebral palsy and an estimated 33 797 across Australia (in 2007). The impact of cerebral palsy is significant, with considerable social and economic costs to the family and the individual (Access Economics 2008).

People with cerebral palsy can have seizures and other impairments affecting their speech, vision, hearing and/or intellect. Worldwide, the incidence of cerebral palsy is the same—one in every 400 births—and, for most, the cause is unknown.

The Spastic Centre offers services to children and adults with cerebral palsy and allied conditions. These services include physiotherapy, speech pathology, occupational therapy, technology, respite, accommodation support, family support, recreation, employment, equipment, recreation, day services and mobility programs.

The organisation also provides education, consultancy and web-based information to clients, the community, service providers and the research and education sectors across Australia and internationally.

The centre has approximately 850 staff and 1000 volunteers at 70 service sites across New South Wales and the Australian Capital Territory.

Knowledge and cerebral palsy

People with cerebral palsy, their families, carers and service providers are on a lifelong quest for knowledge. On diagnosis, families first ask, 'Why did this happen?', then, 'What does the future hold for my child?', then, 'How can I make the best life for my child?' At every stage of their child's life, the family's knowledge needs change. Critical times are around transition points: adjusting to the diagnosis, entering the service system, preschool and school and the transition to adulthood.

No less important are the needs of the growing child—from the time they first ask questions about their disability through to making decisions about their lives as emerging adults. Throughout their adult life, people with cerebral palsy need knowledge of the services and supports that will enable them to lead the best possible life.

Service providers need sound evidence about the interventions that are best suited to each individual. Providers often act as intermediaries, supporting their clients and families by filtering and interpreting the vast array of conflicting information that is increasingly available.

In all instances, a combination of explicit knowledge and tacit knowledge is required

- explicit knowledge: codified knowledge that can be transmitted in formal, systematic language and shared in the form of documents, data, manuals, and so on

- tacit knowledge: personal, context-specific knowledge that is difficult to formalise, record or articulate.It is deeply rooted in individuals' actions and experience as well as in the ideals, values or emotions they embrace (Kidwell et al. 2000).

Knowledge brokering

Knowledge *sharing* is a multi-layered process of exchanging knowledge among individuals and between sectors. Knowledge *brokering* encompasses a range of formal and informal activities and processes undertaken to establish relationships and facilitate effective knowledge exchange (Canadian Health Services Research Foundation n.d.).

The activities of a knowledge broker can include

- developing an understanding of the needs of the different sectors and identifying opportunities for linkages
- bringing individuals and sectors together in knowledge networks to exchange information and work together
- helping groups communicate and understand each other's needs and abilities
- mapping, capturing, translating and distilling knowledge for exchange
- providing the tools for others to capture, transfer, exchange and collaborate around knowledge
- identifying and disseminating best practice
- promoting the use of evidence in funding, planning and delivering services.

Knowledge brokers are entrepreneurial; they are networkers, problem solvers and innovators. They are clear communicators and are perceived as trusted and credible individuals. The role requires an understanding of the cultures of the different environments and they must be able to find and assess relevant knowledge, including research evidence. A knowledge broker is a facilitator, a mediator and a negotiator. They will also love learning and sharing new knowledge (Clarke and Kelly 2005; Canadian Health Services Research Foundation 2003).

Above all, knowledge brokers recognise that knowledge transfer and exchange is a social activity. 'Knowledge depends for its circulation on interpersonal networks, and will only diffuse if these social features are taken into account and barriers overcome' (Greenhalgh et al. 2004:607).

Traditional forms of knowledge brokering at The Spastic Centre

For The Spastic Centre, the traditional sectors or stakeholder groups in the knowledge-sharing and brokering process have comprised: researchers, practitioners (service providers—internal and external) and government policymakers/funders.

The Spastic Centre takes a leadership role within the sector, with a range of knowledge-sharing and brokering initiatives among the research, policy and practitioner communities.

The organisational attributes that contribute to this include

- a culture of innovation, to develop new and creative solutions

- an acknowledgment of the value of every individual and of groups

- a family-centred framework of service delivery, with a strengths-based approach

- an ethos of evidence-based service delivery

- an outward-looking perspective—drawing ideas from a spectrum of sectors

- a record of cultivating national and international networks for support and knowledge sharing

- a strong desire to form partnerships for the benefit of clients and the sector

- a commitment to positively influence the actions, policies and attitudes of government, business and the community.

In recent years, two major projects conducted by The Spastic Centre have strongly utilised knowledge brokering—the first to achieve significant changes in organisational practice and the second in government policy. Both engaged with traditional research/practice/policy stakeholders.

The first project—conducted by The Cerebral Palsy Institute, the research arm of The Spastic Centre—used knowledge brokering to transfer research evidence into practice. This resulted in significant changes to organisational culture, employees' knowledge and management's framework of thinking.

The second project followed the path of service innovation to research, the results of which were brokered to government to achieve changes in public policy.

Research to practice

Evidence-based practice: education with employer support

The following section was written by Dr Iona Novak and describes an example of a knowledge-brokering technique, which was part of a study conducted at The Spastic Centre by staff from The Cerebral Palsy Institute. The study is published elsewhere (Novak et al. 2008; Novak and McIntyre forthcoming).

The 2001–2004 Strategic Plan of The Spastic Centre included a strategy to, 'Introduce an evidence-based approach across all services'. The first stage was to create a culture of research and evidence-based practice within the organisation.

At the commencement of the project, three stakeholders were identified: clients; staff as providers of service; and managers, as decision-makers and leaders, and as the interface between the organisation, government and donors. It was recognised that each group had different needs and strengths, requiring different knowledge strategies.

The knowledge brokering and transfer activities that assisted the cultural shift included:

- Discussions with allied health staff and management about evidence-based practice and its application within a community-based disability service;

- Working with management and the Health Services Union to embed evidence-based practice into allied health role descriptions and linking advanced demonstration of behaviours to remuneration and incentives for promotion; and

- Preparing and presenting a business case to resource internal clinical consultants to take a leadership role in the rollout of evidence-based practice within the organisation, support the knowledge sharing activities and act as evidence-based practice knowledge brokers.

From 2004, the emphasis shifted from changing organisational culture to underpinning all services with evidence. The dual interventions selected to progress this were: knowledge and skill development; and employer support strategies. A range of knowledge sharing and brokering activities were undertaken to support this intervention.

Knowledge and skill development—two key areas were targeted: evidence-based practice and outcome measurement. The two topics are closely interlinked and as a consequence, two parallel research projects were initiated as part of the approach.

Activities included:

- A two-day competency-based training for senior clinical staff on leadership, mentoring and evidence-based practice skills;

- Professional development for junior clinicians led by senior staff and ongoing professional development opportunities under the banner of the CP Institute;

- Development of discipline-specific networks for peer support;

- Support for staff to develop a set of critically appraised topics (CATs) on common interventions; and

- Provision of an evidence alert system to assist practitioners when selecting an intervention to meet the goals of a client or family.

Employer support was also offered. Consultations were held with management to ensure that the activities necessary to implement evidence-based practice and outcome measurement across the organisation were supported and encouraged. Management was also supported to write an interface between evidence-based practice and outcome measurement to embed it, not just as a professional activity, but into service offerings, systems and the processes of service delivery. Senior allied health (Level 3) clinicians were also appointed to take a mentoring role to foster evidence-based practice behaviours across the organisation.

A comprehensive literature review was undertaken at the beginning of the project and two international experts—Margaret Wallen of the Children's Hospital Westmead and Annie McCluskey of the University of Sydney—were consulted about local (NSW) factors that could influence the uptake of evidence-based practice.

Three research projects also ran in parallel with the initiative. Julia Bowman from the University of Western Sydney conducted a randomised control trial that investigated whether education and follow-up mentoring influenced whether or not health professionals used outcomes measurement in practice. Staff members were offered a one-day workshop and follow-up mentoring designed to help them adopt outcome measurement as part of routine practice. Anne Cusick from the University of Western Sydney led two research projects. The first investigated what were the optimal professional development standards recommended in the literature and how the activities of The Spastic Centre compared. The second question examined which occupational-therapy interventions for people with cerebral palsy had the highest levels of research evidence in the literature and how this matched the interventions offered by the organisation. Results from these studies are available in the published literature (Cusick et al. 2009).

Encouragingly, staff at all levels are now taking on roles as catalysts and knowledge brokers—supporting others by sharing knowledge and engaging in collaborative problem solving in mentoring sessions and in internal clinical email groups.

Members of The Spastic Centre's Cerebral Palsy Institute now also provide extensive brokering in the form of consultations and education on the topics of behaviour change in evidence-based practice and outcome measurement to health practitioners and managers in other organisations.

Practice to research to policy

Intensive family support options

The Spastic Centre has a strong record of service innovation. Often, a research project will accompany a new service development to provide sound evidence on its outcomes and effectiveness. With these findings, the knowledge can be shared with the disability service sector and approaches can be made to policymakers and potential funders to extend the offerings of these services across the sector.

One successful example was the Intensive Family Support Options (IFSO) service. The Spastic Centre first offered this service for families who were under such stress that they were requesting an out-of-home placement for their child with a disability. The NSW Government supported the first program under innovative respite service funding.

The service aimed to keep families safely together—with consideration for their physical and emotional wellbeing. The program elements unique to this service were

- short-term (three-month) intensive support
- one therapist worked with each family and was available 24 hours a day and seven days a week, if necessary
- a solution-focused, strengths-based, family-centred (rather than child-centred) approach

- the therapist had a small caseload and offered very practical support

- brokerage funding was available for small household purchases that would make a difference in the families' day-to-day lives (Baldry et al. 2005).

In partnership with the University of New South Wales' School of Social Work, IFSO received an Australian Research Council (ARC) grant to determine 'whether the IFSO program significantly and positively influenced outcomes for the child and family, and if significant positive change did occur, which program elements, strategies and/or techniques significantly contributed to positive client outcomes'.

The study affirmed that the interventions improved families' levels of wellbeing and functioning and were significantly successful in reducing child abuse potential (Baldry et al. 2005).

To extend the knowledge transfer, the IFSO team and the research team from the University of New South Wales presented the findings and service model at a number of national and international conferences and to all referring agencies. They also had extensive consultations with the state government about the effectiveness of the program. In 2005–06, the NSW Government announced funding of $4.1 million under the Intensive Family Support Initiative to establish new services in every region.

It was fortunate that the timing of the brokering efforts coincided with a growing realisation within the disability sector and the government that it was time for a change. Residential facilities were closing and there was increasing recognition that children were better off with their families. The question then became 'how could children be kept safely in the family home'? Although some in the sector had reservations, the strengths-based, solution-focused philosophy and program elements of IFSO were overwhelmingly welcomed as a positive change in approach.

The IFSO project was an example of successful brokering of knowledge about a program—backed by evidence—to policymakers, and now benefiting families across the state.

New landscape of knowledge brokering

In the past five years, The Spastic Centre has recognised the influence of two new stakeholders in the knowledge-brokering arena: consumers and corporations.

The rise of the consumer on the Web

Australians were early adopters of the Internet. Now, 72 per cent of households have home Internet access. Broadband is accessed by 62 per cent of all households in Australia and 86 per cent of all households with Internet access (ABS 2009).

For many years, the World Wide Web has been a source of health information for consumers. In 2000, the Pew Internet and American Life Project reported the Internet's powerful influence on 'health seekers': 55 per cent said that access to the Internet had improved the way they received medical and health information, while 47 per cent of those who sought health information for themselves during their last online search said the material affected their decisions about treatment and care. By 2006, Pew reported that 80 per cent of adults in the United States with Internet access used it for healthcare purposes.

Since 2000, the evolution in communications enabled by the Internet has changed the landscape of knowledge transfer and brokering to and between consumers. In recent years, the Web has changed from an 'expert' model, where information and knowledge were part of a one-way transfer from expert to consumer. Colloquially known as Web 2.0, the Web is now

- social: it is a platform for connecting people

- participatory: the consumer has become the content creator and this is shared peer to peer

- based on groups: formal and informal groups are now easily formed to share information and create new knowledge; many individuals can make small contributions for the greater good

- democratic: web initiatives often have no formal leadership, but rely on catalysts who empower others and then 'leave it to the crowd' (Brafman and Beckstrom 2006)

- global: there is a blurring of national, cultural and sectoral boundaries on the Web (Friedman 2005).

The Web is now the world's largest social network. The Internet has enabled social interactions that go beyond the traditional venues of one's community, work and home settings (Snyder et al. 2006). In 2008, audience measurement company ComScore estimated that the Web had a worldwide audience of 190 858 000 people, while the audience for social networking sites was 131 808 000. In 2007, Technorati was also tracking 70 million weblogs, with approximately 120 000 new weblogs created daily (Sifry 2007).

Yet, as Forkner-Dunn (2003) contends, '[m]ost institutions funding medical research, health policymakers, and health care professionals have ignored both the "e-revolution" and the fact that it is consumer driven'.

A study by Sillence et al. (2006) compared the changes in online health usage between 2000 and 2005. The most popular health topic in 2000 was cancer, while in 2005 it was alternative medicine—'[a] topic little discussed in mainstream healthcare and one which has found a niche online' (Sillence et al. 2006:404). The results also show that people are increasingly seeking personalised health advice. 'Health consumers are searching for sites that match their own social "identity", sites which they feel they can relate to and that are "written for people like themselves"' (Sillence et al. 2006:398).

Changes to The Spastic Centre's approach

Observations of this web-enabled consumer movement influenced The Spastic Centre's 2007–10 strategic plan. The plan includes two outcomes: an expanded range of options for clients and families to connect and reduce isolation, and families which are informed about the best service choice offerings.

Before the development of the plan, a number of online social networking platforms had been identified—blogs, discussion forums, special-interest groups and wikis—where parents of children with a disability not only were connecting with one another for mutual support but appeared to be strongly influencing each other about intervention choices, many of which were not based on evidence. Those engaging in alternative therapies are often very vocal about the perceived benefits for their child. Their credibility is based on the fact that they are *not* professionals, whose practice is grounded in evidence, but rather parents experiencing the same journey as their readers.

In this way, consumers are increasingly making decisions about interventions outside of the evidence-based research/practice/policy realms. Knowledge about this phenomenon was brokered to senior management in the formative stages of the strategic plan. The brokering process involved the identification of web trends, filtering and synthesising this information in light of the expressed needs of the organisation's client base, presentations to senior management and individual negotiation with key managers before the strategic planning process.

The organisation began to consider ways in which parents could be offered mutual support and connection, allowing the 'authentic voice' to be heard while ensuring that the evidence of the best interventions was communicated. Unlike one-way knowledge transfer, this involves knowledge brokering: building personal relationships, facilitating dialogue and debate, understanding the issues for all parties and translating the message for the different audiences.

CP Blogs

A recent major initiative to address this issue is CP Blogs (<www.cpblogs.org.au>). The Spastic Centre has developed it as a place for people with cerebral palsy, their family and friends to come together to share their experiences.

There are four blogs

- *Hey Dad*: written by a father of a child with cerebral palsy, about the day-to-day challenges and unexpected bonuses of having a child with a disability, written from a strengths-based perspective

- *Freefall*: about moving out of home and making a life in the city as a young woman with cerebral palsy; this age group was targeted as many young people have difficulty gaining independence in the transition to adult life

- *Web2Go*: written by a young journalist with cerebral palsy about the technologies and opportunities for engagement on the Web for people with cerebral palsy; in many ways, the Web affords great social potential for people with a disability, as the barriers to physical access and obstacles for people who are non-verbal are less evident in this sphere

- *The Scene*: features news, activities, resources and new research for people with cerebral palsy and their families; *The Scene* was formerly an e-newsletter with a large number of Australian readers.

The blogs are all designed to build a community of readers and to provide quality information for the benefit of people with cerebral palsy and their families. Most importantly, they facilitate the brokering of tacit and explicit knowledge through the blog posts and the provision of a comments function. Knowledge brokering is about conversations. Readers are able to identify with the bloggers as they understand the dichotomy of 'heart' and 'head' that is the journey of cerebral palsy. Readers and bloggers can engage with one another to share their thoughts and debate different perspectives.

The bloggers were all selected for their 'authenticity' (that is, they are people with cerebral palsy or a parent), their ability to write entertainingly and with great insight and their positive, strengths-based approach.

Production standards for the blogs, including design and content, are of a high standard—a barometer of a site's perceived trustworthiness (Sillence et al. 2005). By building a personal reputation in the 'blogosphere', the bloggers might be able to positively influence discussion in online spaces that have not traditionally been the realm of service providers. With trust comes credibility and the influence that this can bring. The Web is filled with proponents of interventions that are not based on evidence. The blog initiatives could assist to redress the balance.

The blogs are also a way to support practitioners to truly understand the issues faced by people with cerebral palsy and their families in a safe (that is, arm's-length) environment. The bloggers are already expressing their opinions about what they find helpful in practice and practitioners have begun to engage in the dialogue through the comments field.

The blogs are linked from The Spastic Centre's 'About cerebral palsy' page, which has an exceptionally high Google results rating: number one in an Australian search for the phrase 'cerebral palsy' and number two in a worldwide search for the phrase. This will attract traffic to the blog site and assist in the communication of the evidence-based messages.

By facilitating knowledge sharing and brokering among people with cerebral palsy and their families, and with practitioners, The Spastic Centre can make one of its most valuable contributions to the lives of its clients. Brokering knowledge gleaned from the 'authentic voice' to practitioners, researchers, policymakers and funders will be a way of placing on the agenda some of the issues that most impact the day-to-day lives of people with cerebral palsy and their families.

Corporate social responsibility

In Australia, corporate community investment is increasingly regarded as a core business activity. In a study reported in *Corporate Community Investment in Australia* (2007), the reasons for this include

- to win and maintain community trust
- to be seen as an employer of choice by staff, particularly young staff who are a major and growing driver of corporate community investment activity
- to broaden the understanding and perspectives of managers and staff
- to build relationships with key stakeholders, including corporate critics.

Sharing and brokering knowledge about the needs and experiences of clients and their families are important ways for not-for-profit organisations to harness support and build partnerships with the corporate sector.

The Spastic Centre's involvement with the corporate sector

The Spastic Centre has strong support from the Australian corporate sector in the areas of service innovation, fundraising for research and voluntary assistance. A number of service developments have been piloted with funding from the sector.

The personal relationships that are developed by the organisation through these networks have led to a number of opportunities to broker knowledge about the needs of people with cerebral palsy that have led to successful outcomes for all stakeholders. High-quality data are matched by personal stories, which can have a powerful impact and are fundamental tools for knowledge brokers (Denning 2006).

Equipment needs and corporate funding

Equipment—such as wheelchairs, walkers and communication devices—is crucial in reducing the impact of cerebral palsy, allowing children and adults to communicate with friends and family, attend school, participate in their community and find employment. In Australia, the cost of meeting therapy and equipment needs has been estimated to be as high as $54.8 million (Australian Institute of Health and Welfare 2006). Although state governments are the largest funders of equipment, there is significant unmet need, with families often seeking funding through community service clubs, small charities or personal fundraising. In 2004, The Spastic Centre began collecting data from its therapists on the unmet need for equipment, including prescription times, waiting lists and outcomes.

At the same time, a major multinational corporate foundation expressed interest in raising money for essential services that would make a significant impact in the lives of people with cerebral palsy.

Knowledge of the unmet need for equipment was brokered to the foundation, together with personal stories of the impact that this was having on the lives of people with cerebral palsy and their families. To address this need, the foundation began an annual fundraising event: a triathlon-style competition between teams comprising some of Australia's major corporations. Since 2004, the event has raised $2 million, which has funded hundreds of items of equipment for children with cerebral palsy.

The partnership and the data on unmet need have drawn the attention of the NSW Government and in 2008 it augmented the funds raised in the event with a $220 000 donation.

Corporate Australia is a powerful ally in addressing the needs of people with a disability. Its increasing interest in practical demonstrations of social responsibility can have direct and systemic benefits. The disability services sector has a role in brokering knowledge about the needs of people with a disability by building continuing relationships with corporations and foundations. Their assistance can take the form of fundraising, volunteering and even knowledge brokering themselves within the corporate and government sectors.

The way ahead

The Spastic Centre is in a unique position to engage in a range of knowledge-brokering activities for the benefit of people with cerebral palsy and their families. A global perspective and a culture of innovation have allowed the organisation to recognise and respond rapidly to the growing influence of consumer and corporate stakeholders among the traditional pillars of research, practice and policy.

With each group, the centre employs a range of knowledge-brokering activities, including

- development of an understanding of the needs of the different sectors and identifying opportunities for linkages
- helping groups communicate and understand each other's needs
- mapping, capturing, translating and distilling knowledge for exchange
- identifying and disseminating best practice
- promoting the use of evidence in funding, planning and delivering services.

The organisation's ability to respond to the changing needs of its stakeholders has been enhanced by its receptivity to information and communications technology, particularly the opportunities it offers for early observation of trends and for knowledge-brokering activities.

Knowledge brokers must be open to values, concepts and exchanges outside the security of their own field. It is crucial to maintain a watching brief on all sectors of the economy and society in order to engage with the ideas and cultivate the diverse external relationships that are at the core of all knowledge-brokering efforts.

Addendum

The Spastic Centre's knowledge-brokering efforts continue, with two recent initiatives using new digital communication and collaboration tools.

ParentWise podcast series

This series of podcasts for families blends research evidence and practical wisdom in a readily accessible form. Written and presented by people who have had many years working with children with a disability, these audiocasts cover such diverse topics as building networks of support, managing a child's behaviour, building resilience, assistive technology options, respite, mealtime issues, a child's growing awareness, siblings and nurturing relationships. The development of the podcasts required a careful brokering process to translate and merge research evidence, clinical practice and the authentic, lived experience of families who had a child with cerebral palsy. The audiocasts and transcripts are available on the web site of the Cerebral Palsy Foundation and on iTunes. CDs of the first series have been distributed to families across the organisation and preloaded iPods made available for loan. The project was made possible through funding by the NSW Department of Human Services, Ageing Disability and Home Care.

Knowledge Hub wiki

The development of a new organisational intranet presented an opportunity to implement a number of social media and collaboration tools. One of the intranet project's aims was to introduce staff to the concept of distributed publishing, in which content experts from around the organisation can create and maintain web site (intranet) pages.

To facilitate this, a wiki (MediaWiki) was integrated into the new intranet. This section, called 'The Knowledge Hub', was designed to gather together information resources but also to be a place where the outcomes of knowledge-brokering efforts could be shared across the organisation.

The first major section of the Knowledge Hub was an Evidence-Based Clinical Decision-Making Library. The project was instigated by The Spastic Centre's Allied Health Consultants and subsequently led and implemented by the centre's Cerebral Palsy Institute. It was designed to support staff at The Spastic Centre to make evidence-based clinical decisions and was part of a broader, multifaceted project to implement a new model of service delivery across the organisation: the Life Needs approach. The development of the content for this section involved a brokering process of collaboratively appraising and translating research evidence—to distil current knowledge in the areas of assessment, intervention and prognosis/prevalence and also develop a set of clinical algorithms. The resources are designed to guide staff to achieve the best possible outcomes, in partnership with clients and families. Studies examining the effectiveness of these approaches, using a randomised controlled trial design are now under way (Campbell et al. 2010).

References

Access Economics 2008, *The economic impact of cerebral palsy in Australia 2007*, April 2008, Report for Cerebral Palsy Australia, Box Hill, Vic., viewed 6 August 2008, <http://www.cpaustralia.com.au/news/access_economics_report.pdf>

Australian Bureau of Statistics (ABS) 2009, *Household Use of Information Technology, Australia, 2008–09*, Australian Bureau of Statistics, Canberra, viewed 1 December 2009, <http://www.abs.gov.au/Ausstats/abs@.nsf/mf/8146.0>

Australian Institute of Health and Welfare 2006, *Therapy and Equipment Needs of People with Cerebral Palsy and Like Disabilities in Australia*, Australian Institute of Health and Welfare, Canberra, viewed 1 June 2007, <http://www.aihw.gov.au/publications/dis/tenpwcplda/tenpwcplda.pdf>

Baldry, E., Bratel, J., Durrant, M. and Dunsire, M. 2005, 'Keeping children with a disability safely in their families', *Practice*, vol. 17, no. 3, pp. 143–56.

Brafman, O. and Beckstrom, R. 2006, *The Starfish and the Spider: The unstoppable power of leaderless organizations*, Penguin Books, New York.

Campbell, L., Novak, I. and McIntyre, S. 2010, 'Patterns and rates of use of an evidence-based practice intranet resource for allied health professionals: a randomised controlled trial', *Developmental Medicine and Child Neurology*, vol. 52, no. S2, p. 31.

Canadian Health Services Research Foundation 2003, *The Theory and Practice of Knowledge Brokering in Canada's Health System*, Canadian Health Services Research Foundation, Ottowa, viewed 10 July 2007, http://www.fcrss.org/brokering/pdf/Theory_and_Practice_e.pdf

Canadian Health Services Research Foundation n.d., *Knowledge Brokering*, Canadian Health Services Research Foundation, Ottawa, viewed 10 July 2007, <http://www.chsrf.ca/keys/use_knowledge_e.php>

Centre for Corporate Public Affairs 2007, *Corporate Community Investment in Australia*, Centre for Corporate Public Affairs, Canberra.

Clark, G. and Kelly, E. 2005, *New Directions for Knowledge Transfer and Knowledge Brokerage in Scotland*, Office of the Chief Researcher, Scottish Executive, Edinburgh, viewed 10 July 2007, <http://www.scotland.gov.uk/Resource/Doc/69582/0018002.pdf>

ComScore 2008, 'Top social networking sites by unique visitors, May 2008', *ClickZ*, viewed 10 July 2008, <http://www.clickz.com/showPage.html?page=3629976>

Cusick, A., Convey, M., Novak, I. and McIntyre, S. 2009, 'Employer-sponsored occupational therapy professional development in a multi-campus facility: a quality project', *Australian Occupational Therapy Journal*, vol. 56, pp. 229–38.

Denning, S. 2006, 'Effective storytelling: strategic business narrative techniques', *Strategy & Leadership*, vol. 34, no. 1, pp. 42–8.

Forkner-Dunn, J. 2003, 'Internet-based patient self-care: the next generation of health care delivery', *Journal of Medical Internet Research*, vol. 5, no. 2 (April–June), viewed 7 June 2007, <http://www.pubmedcentral.nih.gov/articlerender.fcgi?artid=1550561>

Friedman, T. 2005, *The World is Flat: A brief history of the twenty-first century*, Farrar, Straus and Giroux, New York.

Greenhalgh, T., Robert, G., Macfarlane F., Bate, P. and Kyriakidou, O. 2004, 'Diffusion of innovations in service organizations: systematic review and recommendations', *Milbank Quarterly*, vol. 82, no. 4, pp. 581–629, viewed 7 June 2007, <http://www.milbank.org/quarterly/8204feat.html>

Kidwell, J., Vander Linde, K. and Johnson, S. [PricewaterhouseCoopers LLP] 2000, 'Applying corporate knowledge management practices in higher education', *EDUCAUSE Quarterly Articles*, viewed 7 June 2007, <http://connect.educause.edu/Library/EDUCAUSE+Quarterly/ApplyingCorporateKnowledg/39668?time=1218082810>

Novak, I., McIntyre, S., Sharp, N. and Porter, J. 2008, 'Education with employer support improves allied health evidence-based practice knowledge and implementation in a cerebral palsy specialist service', *Developmental Medicine and Child Neurology*, vol. 50, s. 113, p. 43.

Novak, I. and McIntyre, S. (forthcoming), 'Education with workplace supports improves practitioners' evidence based practice knowledge and implementation behaviours', *Australian Occupational Therapy Journal*.

Sifry, D. 2007, 'The state of the live Web, April 2007', *Sifry's Alerts*, viewed 7 June 2008, <http://www.sifry.com/alerts/archives/000493.html>

Sillence, E., Briggs, P. and Fishwick, L. 2005, 'Guidelines for developing trust in health websites', *Proceedings of the International World Wide Web Conference* [poster session], Chiba, Japan, pp. 1026–7, viewed 7 June 2008, ACM Digital Library.

Sillence, E., Briggs, P., Harris, P. and Fishwick, L. 2006, 'Changes in online health usage over the last 5 years', *Proceedings of the 2006 Conference on Human Factors in Computing Systems*, CHI 2006, Montréal, Québec, 22–27 April 2006, ACM 2006, pp. 1331–6, viewed 7 June 2008, ACM Digital Library.

Snyder, J., Carpenter, D. and Slauson, G. 2006, MySpace.com—a social networking site and social contract theory, Paper presented at 2006Proc ISECON conference, Dallas, Texas, viewed 1 March 2008, <http://isedj.org/isecon/2006/3333/ISECON.2006.Snyder.pdf>

4. Making research more relevant to policy: evidence and suggestions[1]

Meredith Edwards

Dimensions of the research–policy problem

Dr Peter Shergold, in launching a book on *Ideas and Influence* (2005), referred to the 'fragility of relationships' as it applies to public policy and the social sciences. He observed that '[t]he relationships between social science and public policy, and between academic and public servant, are ones of the utmost importance'. He went on to say, however: 'They are not, I think, in particularly good shape' (Shergold 2005:2). He elaborated little but could have gone on to mention, as others have (for example, Blunkett 2000), that academic research often deals with issues that are not central to or really relevant to policy debates, and can fail to take the reality of people's lives into account in setting research questions. Conversely, when research tries to be relevant, it can be seen as being driven by ideology dressed up as intellectual inquiry. And a frequent complaint is the lack of timeliness in academic research. Such are the frustrations of many policymakers.

The perspective of academic researchers has been well put by Professors Saunders and Walter in the introduction to their book, *Ideas and Influence* (2005:3): there is a lack of attention by policy practitioners to the subtleties and qualifications of their research findings and a fear that 'those driving policy are seeking to justify actions already decided by "cherry-picking" from among the available evidence with little regard for the robustness or validity of the material selected'. They go on to point out that 'those involved in policy development often have little idea of how or where existing research can contribute, or what is needed to help resolve outstanding issues' (Saunders and Walter 2005:13). To this could be added an anti-intellectual approach sometimes formed within governments; a risk-averse attitude by public servants to findings that could embarrass the

---

1   This chapter was prepared while the author was also chairing a review of the research program of the Australia New Zealand School of Government (ANZSOG). Some of the material in this chapter therefore overlaps that contained in the review document.

minister; the short time frames under which governments operate; and a lack both of respect for the independence of researchers and of incentives needed for researchers to produce policy-relevant material (Edwards 2004:3).

Journalist Paul Kelly (2005:2), in exploring this uneasy relationship, considers the two cultures traditionally foreign worlds; he describes the researcher as the quintessential specialist and the politician as the ultimate generalist. In considering next steps, Kelly (2005:2) goes on: 'Research has got to throw forward to policy. Research has got to be more geared to policy needs, to be effective. The first step on the pathway is to stimulate debate by engaging the policy makers.' Another step he identifies is having a relevant public sector agency involved in the interaction of policymakers and researchers.

So, while the problem of the research–policy nexus is clear, the relationship is quite complex when it comes to being practical about the next steps. A tailored approach, sensitive to the context for each policy problem, is likely to be required if research is to be effectively harnessed; and each issue might require different types of research output or engagement, depending on the stage in the development of policy. Relatedly, the research needed could be descriptive, analytical, diagnostic, theoretical or prescriptive (Solesbury 2002:94). Research could be used directly or simply to raise awareness and start to shape policy thinking through ideas, theories and concepts (Nutley et al. 2007:2). And research can range from traditional academic publications through to a broader interpretation, including, for example, stakeholder consultations and interactive policy/research outputs.

What works best?

Some evidence is starting to emerge about mechanisms that seem to work best for people in the public service who deal with policy issues and who want to engage researchers in solving policy problems. While the evidence to date is not robust, recent work in the United Kingdom by Nutley et al. (2007), based on extensive evaluations, concludes the following about successful research strategies:

> One of the best predictors of research use is…the extent and strength of linkages between researchers and policy makers or practitioners. Personal contact is crucial, which may be informal and *ad hoc*, through email exchanges or telephone conversations, or else more structured and formal, for example at scheduled meetings or shared workshops. We have seen, individual policy makers often rely on a personal network of researchers to identify key findings and as a 'sounding board' for ideas. These interpersonal routes for getting research into policy seem

particularly effective…Above all, however, studies suggest that it is face-to-face interactions that are the most likely to encourage policy and practice use of research. (Nutley et al. 2007:74)

The more traditional linear relationship from research output to policy decisions (and knowledge transfer) is being seen as generally inferior to more interactive approaches to enhancing the use of research; useful research is moving from simply being a stand-alone activity to being part of the policy process.

In addition, the evidence is pointing to

- the value of collective or team approaches in the use of research and decision making as distinct from the tradition of focusing on the output of individual researchers
- the value of intermediation where many voices and agencies are brought into policy processes
- the value of a broader definition of research to encompass a range of types of knowledge generation and dissemination (Nutley et al. 2007).

Some practical suggestions

There are interrelated demand (from governments) and supply (from researchers) issues involved in achieving successful interactions between research and policy, which need to be addressed.

For academics

The way in which people within government bureaucracies operate sometimes has to be seen to be believed! The pace at which they work, the brevity of the briefs they prepare for ministers and the constraints they sometimes face in terms of the ideological framework they need to work within are just a few of the issues they face. Hence, working on secondment within government for a fixed period is an excellent way for academics to gain context and understanding of what is needed if they want to have an influence. The form of secondment could be as an 'academic in residence' on a particular project or in a position that requires greater interaction. Either way, the learning experience can be considerable as well as leading to some influence.

A good example is given below in the case study on 'Working Nation', which deals with the issue of long-term unemployment (LTU), which was of serious policy concern in 1993–94. The case shows the influence of an academic, Professor Bruce Chapman, who had written relevant articles but, importantly, also had developed a network of public servants and political advisers within government who knew of his ideas. These people called on him to take a more active role within government to assist them in bringing labour market policies into action. He worked as a consultant for a time, sat on a key committee and later moved to work as an adviser on labour market issues within the Prime Minister's Office. He returned to academia at the end of the exercise.

For public servants

One of the calls I hear from senior public servants is their problem in accessing relevant knowledge; they need to know who is doing what research and how to access that when they want it. This is the case particularly when the required knowledge crosses disciplines and is needed to assist with whole-of-government issues.

Therefore, some form of intermediary structure or organisation could be needed to act as a broker or a 'clearing house'. Such a 'knowledge-brokering' organisation might assist public servants locate the research or access researchers when needed and could more actively assist in organising round tables involving public servants and academics, if not others, on key policy issues. Being such a 'boundary organisation' is one of the key roles of ARACY.

Other suggestions include: supplementing funding for doctoral students who are researching relevant topics; providing academics with access to government-held data; and bringing in academic experts as well as community representatives to sit on task forces on priority issues. New Zealand has an arrangement whereby researchers are called on to attend forums on emerging issues to assist government 'see above the horizon' on issues they or the researchers choose. In the United Kingdom, there has been some success in seconding outsiders, including academics, to be part of project teams for a specific period (Mulgan 2003:18).

Case study

Nutley et al. (2007:132) discuss at some length five prevalent and important mechanisms for improving the use of research. These often overlap or are used together.

- *Dissemination*: presenting or circulating research findings targeted to the potential audience.
- *Interaction*: developing stronger links and collaborations across the sectors.

- *Social influence*: relying on those with influence, such as experts and peers, to inform and persuade individuals about the research and its value.

- *Facilitation*: enabling the use of research, whether that is technically, financially or in other ways.

- *Incentives and reinforcements*: using rewards and other means to reinforce desired behaviours.

These mechanisms, particularly the first three, certainly proved important to me when I was Deputy Secretary in the Department of Prime Minister and Cabinet and chaired a task force of officials in 1993–94 involved in developing the 'Working Nation' package of measures. In writing up this case study (Edwards 2001:176), I noted as a concluding observation that 'especially crucial in this case was the role of academics in producing policy-relevant knowledge on the nature and dimensions of the LTU [long-term unemployment] problem'.

In this case study, the influence of knowledge transfer from academic (and other non-government) research to practice can be seen best in the early stages of the development of policies after the election in 1993—particularly in

- identifying the problem and getting the issue of long-term unemployment on the political agenda

- the stage of policy analysis: collecting and analysing data, identifying key issues and formulating relevant options.

Problem identification

Several factors led to the issue of long-term unemployment being put firmly on the agenda, but a crucial contribution came from three ANU academics who drew attention to the urgency of the problem. Two of the researchers were the 'producers' of the knowledge (Junankar and Kapuscinksi). The third, Professor Bruce Chapman, wrote about the issue but also was key to its dissemination. The dissemination occurred effectively because Chapman was part of a network of people he had met in 'earlier lives', through his involvement as 'architect' of the Higher Education Contribution Scheme (HECS) and who now were influential in ministerial offices and in the relevant department. Immediately after the Keating government's victory in the 'un-winnable election' in 1993, those in this network of people were talking to each other (see Edwards 2001:14 ff. for more detail; for Chapman's role, see Appendix 4.1).

Before moving to the Department of Prime Minister and Cabinet, I was in the then Department of Employment, Education and Training (DEET) running the Economic Analysis Division. I could see that senior people within the department and most ministerial staff needed some convincing of the seriousness of the problem. Chapman was invited to present his findings at a seminar of carefully selected people, including the head of the department, his deputies and relevant ministerial advisers, including from the Prime Minister's Office. The way in which Chapman presented the case with his analysis and graphs certainly convinced our Secretary and his deputies. Processes snowballed from there, including DEET hiring Chapman as a consultant to write up the issue in more detail, especially about who were the long-term unemployed—a gap in our knowledge at the time.

Policy analysis

This was not a process involving the usual interdepartmental committees. Instead, a high-level committee, the Committee on Employment Opportunities (CEO), was set up within the Department of Prime Minister and Cabinet (PM&C) to oversee the policy to alleviate long-term unemployment. Its membership was critical to its success. The committee, reporting to the Prime Minister, could not afford to come up with solutions at odds with the broad direction of government policy, so it was chaired by the Secretary of the Department of PM&C, Dr Michael Keating, and a senior policy adviser within the Prime Minister's Office was on it. It also included two other heads of department, one member of the non-government sector and two academics, with Chapman as an observer. It was served by a task force, which I headed and which had as its first main task identifying gaps in knowledge on the nature and composition of long-term unemployment and attempting to fill them, including commissioning papers from academic researchers and community groups, such as the Brotherhood of St Laurence and the Australian Council of Social Services (ACOSS).

One excellent example of the interaction of the sectors occurred between Treasury officials and the academics on the CEO on a purely technical but politically significant issue on which there was no hard evidence. There was considerable disagreement on the extent to which government intervention to assist the long-term unemployed would reduce the unemployment rate. A one-day workshop in which there was intense debate between bureaucrats and academics followed (for more detail, see Edwards 2001:153–4). Chapman's assessment of this process was:

> In terms of the relevance of research to the policy process, this was a critical example...Things would have gone quite differently if we had not had the technical expertise to present these arguments, and if Treasury had had the superior expertise to destroy our arguments. It was a very academic exercise, but behind this, politics and ideology were critical. (In Edwards 2001:154)

More examples from this case study could be given of the benefits of interaction between academic researchers (working from the outside as well as inside of government), on the one hand, and senior officials, on the other; and of the important role of business, unions and community groups, as well as the unemployed themselves, in interacting with government in the policy process. The above examples should suffice, however, to illustrate the importance of dissemination and interaction in the research process, as well as the benefits of influence through established networks.

It could be argued that circumstances were favourable to using research in this case given that the demand side—that is, the government—was responsive. That certainly helped, but does not detract from the need to look beyond the academic article and beyond the linear process of transferring knowledge for effective impact.

Conclusion

It is not much use producing knowledge that could be relevant if it is not also effectively disseminated. Yet many academics are focused on producing articles and then lose interest beyond that point, preferring to move onto the next article, despite potential policy or practitioner relevance. Therefore there is a need for many forms of intermediary agencies to connect producers to users. A linear relationship between these two—as this chapter has demonstrated—might not be sufficient, however, if there is to be policy influence from researchers. Interactive processes seem to be a key ingredient.

Interaction in developing policy increasingly needs to include groups other than academic researchers. Although this chapter has focused mainly on the relationship between academics and public servants, the importance of the interaction of both these sets of players with broader community interests should not be neglected. In the case study above, community and business groups were important in research and the consultation process. In an environment of more engagement by governments with their communities, academics cannot afford *not* to be closely in tune with citizen views if they wish to influence policy and practice.

Appendix 4.1

Recollections of Labor policy advisers, March 1993

Bruce Chapman, academic seconded into government

> I can remember Tom Burton, the journalist, calling me up and asking me what happened the day after the election...I can remember phone calls with various people—Mary Ann [O'Loughlin], maybe Meredith [Edwards], certainly David Phillips—who said we must do something about long-term unemployment. They knew it was there; maybe they were getting information from the department as well as other people from Keating's office, but it had to be addressed. But because they had seen me as so involved in the research side they wanted to discuss the possibility of something happening. My involvement started with personal liaison with those people. David Phillips said, 'Bring all your pictures that you have been complaining about to me and to Mary Ann and Meredith, and come and have dinner with [Employment Minister, Kim] Beazley', which I did, and they explained why long-term unemployment was an economic issue.

Mary Ann O'Loughlin, social policy adviser to Prime Minister Paul Keating

> The Sunday after the election I thought, if Bruce Chapman is right, then we—meaning the government—are politically in deep, deep trouble. By the time of the next election, long-term unemployment would be terrible—even if the recovery came through, even if short-term unemployment lifted up, long-term unemployment would be sticking out like the proverbial sore thumb; and for a Labor government that is about the worst thing you can get: this would be particularly bad on the Labor Government's credentials. So it is definitely Bruce's work that put this issue on the agenda and definitely a political imperative about winning an election.

David Phillips, senior adviser to Kim Beazley, Minister for Employment, Education and Training.

> Very early on I had the sense that we had won the unwinnable election and we had gone into that election almost silent on unemployment. We had cobbled together a bit of a policy but we all knew that it was inadequate. So I and obviously others, had a very strong sense that something had to be done about that now that we had won. I rang Bruce

quite early in the piece and simply said 'What have you been doing on unemployment and long-term unemployment?' I can remember trying to draw the Beveridge Curve as he described it to me over the telephone. He said 'You can shift it to the left or the right...' I then either spoke to Mary Ann or I had another conversation with Bruce, but that set the ball rolling. The significance of the Beveridge Curve was not so much any of the theory behind it but the fact that here there was, for the first time, an argument that said there can be positive economic returns from doing something about long-term unemployment.

Adapted from Edwards (2001:145–6).

References

Australia New Zealand School of Government (ANZSOG) Research Reference Group 2007, *Enhancing ANZSOG's Contribution to Better Government: Future research directions*, October, Australia New Zealand School of Government, The Australian National University, Canberra, viewed 3 May 2010, <http://www.anzsog.edu.au/content.asp?pageId=21>

Blunkett, David 2000, Influence or irrelevance: can social science improve government?, Speech to a meeting convened by the Economic and Social Research Council, February.

Edwards, Meredith 2001, *Social Policy, Public Policy: From problem to practice*, Allen & Unwin, Crows Nest, NSW.

Edwards, Meredith 2004, *Social science research and public policy: narrowing the divide*, Policy Paper 2, Academy of the Social Sciences in Australia, Canberra.

Kelly, Paul 2005, Presentation to ARACY Conference, 12 August.

Mulgan, Geoff 2003, Government, knowledge and the business of policy making, Keynote address to Facing the Future: Engaging stakeholders and citizens in developing public policy, National Institute for Governance Conference, Canberra, April.

Nutley, S., Walter, I. and Davies, H. 2007, *Using Evidence: How research can inform public services*, Policy Press, Bristol.

Saunders, Peter and Walter, James 2005, *Ideas and Influence*, UNSW Press, Sydney.

Shergold, Peter 2005, 'Book launch at annual symposium', *Dialogue* [Academy of the Social Sciences], vol. 24, no. 3.

Solesbury, William 2002, 'The ascendancy of evidence', *Planning Theory and Practice*, vol. 3, no. 1.

5. KnowledgExchange: a knowledge-brokering initiative in the Victorian child and family welfare sector

Cathy Humphreys and Richard Vines

Introduction

> As the diameter of our knowledge increases, the circumference of our ignorance expands. (Anonymous stem-cell researcher)[1]

The words used by the anonymous stem-cell researcher could apply equally to the challenges of knowledge brokering in the children and families sector. Our knowledge base in the area is undoubtedly increasing; however, the ability to translate and use aspects of this knowledge base in practice in ways that make a difference to the lives of children and young people and their families remains a constant challenge.

This chapter initially describes a broad-based knowledge-brokering initiative in Victoria. It then concentrates on one aspect of this program: the way in which the information technology infrastructure for the sector and particularly the practices of managers and front-line workers using electronic data systems can be brokered to more usefully inform practice. It raises the question of whether these systems are barriers to or facilitators of good practice in the area. This is a question that has been addressed eloquently by Parton (2008), who questions whether social work and particularly child protection practice are being shifted from the 'terrain of the social' to the 'terrain of the informational'. This project used a knowledge broker (RV) to explore these changes in practice with front-line workers and managers.

While the primary goal of the project was to explore the role that an understanding of organisational data could play in supporting practice with vulnerable children and their families, it also raised the broader question of the interface between workers, managers, consumers and the technology of

---

1 We are grateful to Nick Collins, formerly with Glastonbury Child and Family Services, for making us aware of this quotation.

electronic databases. The conceptual question is whether electronic databases are simply electronic versions of a paper file. This would suggest a first-order change in which there is merely the imposition of a different technology to support the same work with the goal (not always realised!) of an increase in efficiency (Ison and Russell 2000). Alternatively, the scale of technological advances could be such that a second-order change is occurring that shifts the nature of practice—as Parton (2008) suggests is now occurring. Second-order changes go beyond the question of efficiency ('how' to work better) to look at questions of purpose ('what' are we doing and 'why') (Checkland and Poulter 2006). The question then arises of how this shift can be used to enhance rather than undermine the interventions and the outcomes for vulnerable children and families. It is a critical question in which we feel a knowledge broker has a key role to play.

The KnowledgExchange initiative

Before focusing on the particular information technology project initiated by the knowledge broker, situating the work within its broader context provides an explanation for how this somewhat unusual knowledge-brokering project arose as part of a relationship between the Alfred Felton Chair in Child and Family Social Work and the Centre for Excellence in Child and Family Welfare.

The chair was established as a collaborative initiative between the Alfred Felton Trust, the Social Work Department at the University of Melbourne and the peak body for 95 member organisations in the child, youth and family services sector in Victoria. The role of the new chair was conceptualised as contributing to the knowledge base for the children and families sector in Victoria with a particular emphasis on capacity building in the community-sector organisations. Two aims were associated with this particular chair: the development of new and relevant research to inform practice and policy; and the implementation of current knowledge already developed, but under-utilised by the sector.

The second aim was supported by the employment for three years of a knowledge broker through a successful application by the centre to the Telstra Foundation. Work progressed to support a knowledge-brokering agenda for the centre and the chair in this collaborative initiative now branded 'KnowledgExchange'. The collaborative arrangement is depicted in Figure 5.1. Conceptions of the knowledge-brokering role itself have been influenced by the experience of those involved in the early stages of the project. For example, the knowledge broker was recruited from outside the community sector. He has contributed to an overall team approach that has shaped the project agenda by integrating perspectives derived from previous and practical experiences associated with knowledge management (Vines and Naismith 2002), including complex and technical matters associated with print and electronic text convergence (Vines 2006; Printing Industries Association of Australia 2004; RMIT 2004).

Figure 5.1 Links between the Alfred Felton Research Program, the Centre for Excellence and the KnowledgExchange project

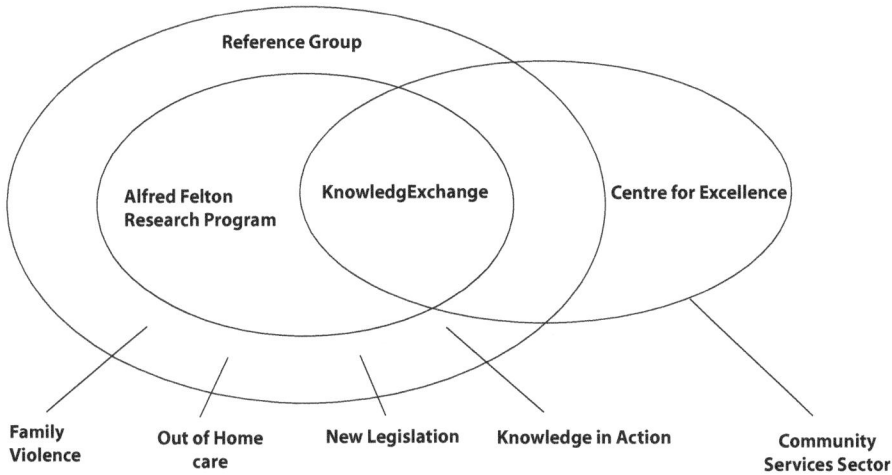

The Alfred Felton Research Program receives input from a reference group on four areas: family violence, out-of-home care, new legislation and knowledge in action.

Thanks to Jenny Higgins, the second knowledge broker for the KnowledgExchange project, for the figure.

At the heart of the KnowledgExchange agenda is the intention to impact on the lives of vulnerable children and their families primarily through the knowledge development of practitioners and their managers. The objective of the KnowledgExchange is to develop three key themes

- to deepen the culture of evidence-informed decision making within the child and family welfare sector

- to create an environment in which innovation can flourish within the existing networks of influence and activities being developed under the umbrella of the Centre for Excellence and the Alfred Felton Research Program headed by the chair

- to facilitate the sharing of practice wisdom and organisational knowledge within the children, youth and families sector in Victoria.

The project is assisted by the collaborative infrastructure provided by the two participating institutions. The centre provides advocacy, professional development, research, training, policy and program advice, publications and resources for the 95 participating community-sector organisations. The chair brings research and research utilisation expertise. Together, through a process of extensive consultation in the sector and with the help of a reference group of key stakeholders, three strands of work have been identified as priority areas. It is envisaged that each of the three strands will provide rich themes for the exploration of original research as well as the development of the KnowledgExchange project facilitated by the knowledge broker.

The first of the three strands of work is *supporting earlier intervention with vulnerable children and their families* through working with the Victorian family support initiative known as Child FIRST (which stands for Family Information, Referral and Support Team). This provides coordinated, community-based intake and family support to vulnerable children and families through a range of community-sector organisations. The initiative is supported by the *Children, Youth and Families Act, 2005*, which brings new ways of working into the family support-sector organisations. Two themes in this complex project have been highlighted

- The knowledge base for partnership working. New organisational forms of working are now emerging (and being imposed). The knowledge base to inform partnerships and network development is still embryonic, yet has a role to play in informing more efficient and effective forms of organisation for delivering services to children and their families.

- The use of data to inform and develop practice. This theme is progressively expanding to take in the broader facilitation of a strategic approach to community-sector organisation support systems infrastructure such as client information management, records management and web publishing. It is this aspect of the KnowledgExchange project that is the focus of the case study later in this chapter.

Family violence and its practice development within family support services is the second strand of work. In the past, intervention in this area has been provided primarily by family violence specialist workers. A new 'whole-of-government' strategy for Victoria configures family services organisations, Child FIRST and a network of mainstream health and welfare organisations working together to deliver services. This requires significant new knowledge, particularly for those organisations in the children and families sector that have not traditionally engaged with this issue. Drawing this knowledge into family support services serves a range of agendas. One is developing a more informed workforce to intervene in the complex issues of family violence in collaboration with other key organisations.

The third strand of work—*supporting quality and stability for children in out-of-home care*—is a particular priority and driver in the new children, youth and families legislation in Victoria. A number of projects are developing. For example, of relevance to this chapter has been the establishment of a seeding project funded through the University of Melbourne's 'Knowledge Transfer' program (University of Melbourne 2007). This initial and small-scale project has emerged through collaboration between the University's eScholarship Research Centre, the Alfred Felton Chair and the Centre for Excellence and forms part of a network of integrated knowledge-brokering initiatives. This particular intervention has been developed to bring to the surface the significant reform challenges associated with electronic data systems and other forms of record keeping for children and young people in out-of-home care. The 'Who Am I?' project has subsequently developed as an ARC Linkage project. This is providing a focus for consolidating the university's KnowledgExchange project and a range of other initiatives and aims to link past and present through highlighting the significance of record keeping and information management in the digital world. As part of this project, archivists and historians propose a new resource to support the accessibility of information about Victorian child welfare institutions and where record holdings are kept (<www.pathwaysvictoria. info>).

It is envisaged that the development of the KnowledgExchange project will underpin each of these strands of research, though the real configuration for each will take a different form, depending on the stakeholders involved in each project and the priorities they have in bridging the gaps between research, policy and practice. In this process, we have been assisted by the International Symposium in 2008 held in Dartington, England (<www.ripfa.org.uk>), which explored five different dimensions of knowledge-brokering work

- strategies for identifying evidence (the role of the literature review and meta-analysis)
- strategies for delivering evidence-informed practice
- supporting and exploring the role of in-house evaluation
- strategies for embedding evidence-informed practice
- strategies for evaluating the impact of a knowledge-brokering project (how do we know we are making a difference?).

Conceptually, the work draws on the cultures-in-context model of research use (Arney and Bromfield 2008). The model attempts to understand the different cultures of research, policy and practice within the context of wider domains of influence. Within this context, research and evidence are theorised as only two of many drivers that shape policy and practice. The knowledge broker sits within this context 'spanning' the different domains, scanning the emergent practices and policies and constructing opportunities to create strategies for the enhanced use of research in policy and practice. The five different dimensions of knowledge-brokering work provide the framework for or tool-kit of strategies from which the broker can draw in this 'spanning' work.

The project to explore the role of data systems in developing evidence-informed practice initially arose within the strand of 'early intervention'. It was here, in the new Child FIRST partnerships developed between different family service providers and statutory child protection (Victorian Department of Human Services), that the focus on the role of databases first arose as a 'live' issue for interrogation and exploration. The ramifications for out-of-home care and domestic and family violence also quickly emerged.

Case study: exploring the use of data systems to develop evidence-informed practice

It is unsurprising in the Victorian children, youth and families sector that interest in the electronic databases used by family services workers to support their practice can be galvanised. The 'Every Child Every Chance' reform in this sector, which resulted in a new systems configuration for child protection and family services, was driven partly by a careful analysis of the statutory child protection database in 2002. The analysis of these organisational data showed that: 60 per cent of notifications to child protection were re-notifications; an increasing number of notifications were closed with 'no further action' at intake; and the adult issues of domestic violence, mental illness and problematic substance use featured in more than 70 per cent of cases and yet the child protection system was not designed to respond to these complex issues. Moreover, it was predicted that within 10 years, one in five children in Victoria would come to the notice of this system, which was clearly failing to respond appropriately to their needs or to those of their parents and other family members (Allen Consulting 2003).

While other factors were also significant in driving the reform, the attention to evidence drawn from these administrative databases provides a continuing story that is well known within the Victorian Government and non-government sector. It provides a context in which the power of evidence to support reform has been demonstrated.

In spite of this history, however, the engagement between practitioners, managers and these organisational databases is complex. Consultation with front-line workers, community-sector organisation managers and researchers in the children and family services area by the chair and knowledge broker consistently raised the ubiquitous and contentious nature of the electronic data systems used by front-line workers. It also raised an interesting challenge for the definition of knowledge brokering given that the role of databases and data mining is generally conceptualised as part of a research agenda. Nevertheless, it is also a 'boundary-spanning' issue in that organisational data can provide direct knowledge to inform policy and practice. How databases are used, the opportunities and the limitations provided by the current databases and the impact on practice lent themselves to an aspect of KnowledgExchange— namely, the sharing of practice wisdom and organisational knowledge within the children, youth and families sector in Victoria. Generally, we would envisage attention to organisational databases and their use as fitting broadly within the strategies for delivering evidence-informed practice. The focus on the capacity to use data and information to monitor patterns at multiple levels within complex systems (including team, organisation, catchment, regional and state-wide levels) is, however, a particular subcategory of knowledge-brokering work.

A starting point for the initiative was created by a practice forum and a 'twilight seminar series' at which practitioners, managers and researchers were invited to present and discuss data issues that were impacting on practice. Slightly bemused practitioners, managers and academics wondered together about how the role of electronic databases could be such an engaging topic at five o'clock in the afternoon.

A number of issues emerged across the seminar series. It became clear that while electronic systems were accepted as a central part of human services practice, in their current form they were constantly problematised. The issues raised included

- the alienation of front-line workers from the data they input, which provide little feedback to them to inform their practice, and instead generally seem to be used by others

- the inadequacy of the designated fields (data elements) in the electronic data system, which might not reflect the context-specific work undertaken with the children and their families

- the lack of compliance by workers, which means that the data might not reflect their real work or the work of the organisation

- double handling of client information if paper-filing (analogue) systems are required in parallel with the electronic client information management (digital) systems, or where compliance requires logging information into two or more different electronic management systems

- the amount of time spent by workers at their computers, which, it is claimed, detracts from working with clients

- the ethical issues raised by the automatic information sharing that can occur through the electronic data system—a particular issue when the statutory and non-government sectors share the same electronic data system

- the multiple electronic data systems used by any one organisation, which do not interface with each other and which do not allow the community-sector organisation to gain an overall picture of their work

- the sustainability of the electronic record into the future. A particular issue relates to those leaving care, who might want to access information about themselves and the organisational context in which they lived at a later date.

Presentations were not, however, entirely negative. An optimistic and progressive use for the state-wide databases lay in their potential to provide back to the sector meaningful reports about trends in family services practice at the state-wide and regional or catchment levels, as long as resources were provided for such analysis (Boffa 2007). Similarly, the creation of purpose-built databases was also providing meaningful data for some organisations, supporting their processes of referral and intake, as well as providing useful information on 'demand flow'.

In raising these issues in the seminar series, as well as at community forums and reference group meetings, a range of issues that coalesce around the information technology systems within each community-sector organisation has begun to be explored. A further step will now be taken with a one-day conference that will investigate the implications for community-sector organisations building their own custom-made systems, buying or sharing those developed by other organisations or relying on inputting into the government databases.

The next stages in this process of exploration are now occurring in an attempt to address some of the issues that had been problematised through the knowledge broker and practitioner-led seminar series. The successful research multi-agency application ('Who Am I?') to the ARC continues the exploration of the ways in which the electronic data are to be archived for those leaving care. A data-user group has also been established with the assistance of one of the presenters in the seminar series (Julie Boffa), a worker who spans social work and database analysis. Data reports arising from the network of Child FIRST consortia are being used to interpret and understand 'the flow of work' through networks in Victoria.

The establishment of this data-user group, which meets as part of the Child FIRST practitioner and manager forum, allows for analysis of quarterly reports as they become available. Aggregated reports from the Department of Human Services database are provided to the Child FIRST and family service alliances to show a state-wide overview. In addition, there are local government area and catchment-level reports, which provide the data at this level of aggregation allowing networks to understand the picture of work for their area.

The benefits for participants include

- the development of an understanding of the local and state patterns reported through an analysis of the data reports

- the ability to examine trends in data over time

- understanding both the strengths and limitations of the data, and how and whether they accurately reflect the practitioner and management experience of the work of the Child FIRST networks

- understanding about how the data can be fed back to managers and practitioners to inform the development of practice in Child FIRST networks.

We believe such an initiative has important potential. It can provide a catalyst for a more substantial partnership framework between the community-sector organisations and the Victorian Government. If such a collaborative mechanism can develop that results in the joint monitoring of emergent patterns of behaviour within the child and family welfare sector as a whole (Vines 2007), this could usher in a new approach to community capacity formation. It would also begin to address the processes through which front-line workers and managers are able to mine and analyse their own data to provide a more evidence-informed practice and an understanding of their place in patterns that emerge across the state.

The continuing exploration of the ways in which the information requirements of the sector and government are shifting and changing the nature of work with children and families creates another level of analysis for practitioners, managers and academics (Parton 2008). This is an intensely theoretical as well as practical issue, which points to the changing nature of our work in the 'electronic and digital era'. It creates a much-needed focus on the importance of information and communication technology systems as an integral part of creating linkages (or barriers) between policy personnel, practitioners and researchers. It is an issue that is both marginal (as a legitimate topic in children and families work) and central (as a time-consuming and mandated aspect of most children and families practice).

Conclusion

The KnowledgExchange initiative provides opportunities to span the boundaries between different and often siloed cultures of research, practice and policy. In this process, academics, community-sector organisations and government workers are provided with opportunities to engage with knowledge sharing and problem solving. The project is informed by the 'cultures-in-context' model, which recognises that research and new knowledge are emergent and based on scanning for and creating opportunities for exchange within the worlds of research, policy and practice (Arney and Bromfield 2008). The initiative also recognises that an evidence-informed practice emerges when engaged practitioners and managers share their current practice in the context of an open inquiry in which research is one of several sources of new knowledge.

References

Allen Consulting 2003, *Protecting Children: The child protection outcomes project*, September, Department of Human Services, Government of Victoria, Melbourne.

Arney, F. and Bromfield, L. 2008, Strategies for delivering evidence informed practice: solutions not problems, Beyond the Rhetoric International Symposium, Dartington, UK, April 2008, viewed 3 May 2010, <http://www.aifs.gov.au/institute/pubs/papers/papers08.html>

Boffa, J. 2007, Advancing the Child FIRST reforms through meaningful data, Seminar Series: Data Systems to Support Evidence Informed Practice, University of Melbourne and Centre for Excellence in Child and Family Welfare, 28 June 2007.

Checkland, P. and Poulter, P. 2006, *Learning for Action: A short definitive account of soft systems methodology and its use for practitioner, teachers and students*, Wiley & Sons, Chichester, UK.

Ison, R. and Russell, D. 2000, *Agricultural Extension and Rural Development: Breaking out of knowledge transfer traditions*, Cambridge University Press, UK.

Parton, N. 2008, 'Changes in the form of knowledge in social work: from the "social" to the "informational"', *British Journal of Social Work*, vol. 38, pp. 253-269.

Pathways 2009, Pathways web site, viewed 3 May 2010, <http://www.pathwaysvictoria.info/index.html>

Printing Industries Association of Australia 2004, *Business Insights: Key learnings arising from EPICS projects, 2000–2004*, Printing Industries Association of Australia, Newmarket, Qld, viewed 3 May 2010, <http://www.printnet.com.au/.../industry_reports_sub_pages/business_insights__key_learnings_from_epics.html>

Royal Melbourne Institute of Technology (RMIT) 2004, *The C-2-C Project: Creator to consumer in a digital age*, Royal Melbourne Institute of Technology, Vic., viewed 27 March 2010, <http://c-2-cproject.com/background_html>

University of Melbourne 2007, *Knowledge Transfer: Connecting Melbourne*, University of Melbourne, Vic., p. 24, viewed 3 May 2010, http://web.archive.org/web/20080719030202/http://www.knowledgetransfer.unimelb.edu.au/KT_NOV07_webversion.pdf

Vines, R. 2006, *From In-House Printing to Document Workflow. A guide for the better serving of readers, users and knowledge workers in an era of communications and digital media convergence*, Canon Australia, North Ryde, NSW, viewed 3 May 2010, <http://www.nippa.com.au/pdf/RichardVinesJune06.pdf>

Vines, R. 2007, *Towards a futures strategy for the Victorian community services sector: a knowledge perspective*, VCOSS Congress Paper, August 2007, viewed 3 May 2010, <http://www.vcoss.org.au/documents/VCOSS%20docs/Congress/2007/Presentations/B1%20VINES.pdf>

Vines, R. and Naismith, L. 2002, 'Exploring the foundations of knowledge management practice', in B. Cope and R. Freeman (eds), *Developing Knowledge Workers in the Printing and Publishing Industries: Education, training and knowledge management in the publishing supply chain, from creator to consumer*, Common Ground, Melbourne, viewed 3 May 2010, <http://richardvines.cgpublisher.com/product/pub.174/prod.1>

6. The art and science of influence: reflections from the boundary

Sharon Goldfeld

In Malcom Gladwell's book *The Tipping Point: How little things can make a big difference* (2002), he outlines how focusing on a number of key principles can assist in using evidence-based ideas (for example, the effects of climate change) to create social change. These three principles are centred on: 1) the law of the few—social change is often heavily dependent on a few people who are leaders, assisted by others who connect with and transmit the message; 2) the 'stickiness factors'—special characteristics of a message that render it so memorable that the message 'sticks'; and 3) the power of context—the idea that people are more sensitive to the influence of their environment or context (as opposed to individual character traits) than has previously been thought. Gladwell emphasises that social change requires an iterative process, with attention to detail around all three of the core principles. Through these three principles, Gladwell has, perhaps unwittingly, outlined what could be thought of as the core processes that help underpin the role of the knowledge broker as a key agent of change.

Gladwell's approach offers a useful framework for reflecting on the processes that might be necessary for effective knowledge brokering to capitalise on the research/policy nexus. In transferring this approach into the policy context, there is therefore the need for: 1) developing the evidence-based memorable message; 2) an understanding of the political context (the power of context); and 3) the ability to influence leadership. While many authors have analysed and considered the limited *science* of knowledge brokering, it could be that in order to effect real change the *art* of influence must be given equal attention.

In order to build on Gladwell's thinking, the starting point for this chapter has to be a better understanding of what knowledge brokering might mean in the current political and policy context in Australia and internationally. This requires not only an explanation and discussion of the definitions of knowledge brokering, but also a reflection on the skills that might be necessary for knowledge brokers in order to influence social change—particularly for children—in the current policy and political environment. This chapter will focus on examples of knowledge-brokering processes that have attempted to influence outcomes for children and families. It is written from the perspective of someone in the somewhat unusual position of having a 'foot in two camps': a part-time postdoctoral research and clinical position and a policy position in a government department.

What is a knowledge broker?

There are now a number of terms being used to describe the general process of bringing together the research and policy worlds. While the terminology is relatively recent, the idea of researchers actively influencing policy has a long tradition, reaching well back into the annals of public health research. In the past, research has at times had a profound influence on policy and the subsequent funding of infrastructure, thereby improving the lives of hundreds of thousands of children—for example, John Snow's research into cholera transmission and the subsequent closure of the Broad Street water pump (Snow 1885). Today, in the developed world, the change processes appear to be more complex and incremental, the 'research ammunition' for influence less dramatic and the policy levers for change disconnected from where the final benefits emerge (for example, quality preschooling associated with decreased crime) (National Research Council Institute of Medicine 2000). Nevertheless, there are still substantial opportunities for research to benefit the present and future lives of children.

The following definitions from the Canadian Health Services Research Foundation (CHSRF) have merged from the relatively recent (historically speaking) surge in interest in evidence-based practice and policymaking (Bronson et al. 2006) and the need to make more explicit an understanding of the processes and roles considered necessary for success.

The CHSRF has an international reputation as a leader in knowledge transfer—more recently renamed 'knowledge exchange'. It describes knowledge exchange as the 'interaction between decision makers and researchers that results in mutual learning through the process of planning, producing, disseminating, and applying existing or new research in decision-making'. The CHSRF separates knowledge exchange from knowledge brokering, which it describes as 'supporting evidence-based decision-making in the organization, management, and delivery of health services'. Knowledge brokering is, then, the active process that links researchers and decision makers (or practitioners) so that they are better able to 'understand each other's goals and professional culture, influence each other's work, forge new partnerships, and use research-based evidence' (Canadian Health Services Research Foundation 2008). Knowledge brokering seems necessary for knowledge exchange. The key link for these processes is the knowledge broker: the individual or organisation that facilitates action.

A difficulty with these definitions is that their apparent simplicity belies the complexity of the process in real terms. These definitions also—perhaps for the sake of brevity—ignore the importance of the need for change as a key process driver. It can be argued that knowledge transfer or exchange processes facilitate change best when there is a clear goal in sight, with a strategy that articulates how the knowledge broker can use these processes to act as an agent of social change. The role of the knowledge broker is therefore shifted from a potentially passive or facilitative role to that of a driver of change, requiring a number of skills including the capacity to communicate across professional paradigms, to understand different contexts and to utilise opportunistic change when it arises. In a review of the theory and practice of knowledge brokering, the CHSRF (2003) outlines the skill set necessary or desirable for knowledge brokering. This includes

- the capacity to gather and critically appraise evidence
- the ability to see the 'big picture'
- good communication and mediation skills
- curiosity and listening skills.

These suggest that the knowledge broker requires a specific set of skills that is different from those needed by researchers in general, although clearly building on a set of common competencies. The real strength of knowledge brokering is the ability to understand both sides of the policy and research worlds, preferably in terms of content and process. Knowledge brokers also need skills in the art of persuasion. These skills alone, however, are not sufficient and could lead to inappropriate policy action—for example, when lobby groups for specific narrow interests are able to influence policy. The knowledge broker must therefore also have the skills to understand, categorise and synthesise evidence and research to ensure that the best research is informing policy, while at the same time understanding which policy levers are best suited to implement change. This is the cutting edge of knowledge brokering and suggests that the most successful knowledge brokers are those who have the capacity to bring together the art and science of influence to effect change.

Environments that facilitate knowledge brokering

The policymaking environmental context is an important one to consider for successful knowledge brokering. Policy environments can often change rapidly. Figure 6.1 outlines the aspects of the policy environment that enable change when they co-occur. For example, Kingdon (1995) argues that in order to open a policy window and influence the decision-making agenda, three separate yet linked ideas need to come together at a critical time. These are recognition of a problem (data), identification of a potential solution pathway within a policy framework (evidence-based strategies) and a political imperative where there is potential for commitment and the constraints are not too severe. These then support the broader constructs that Moore (2007) suggests are necessary for governments to perform well—namely: 1) capability (for example, personnel, skills, infrastructure); 2) a notion of public value in the change processes and results (important for political will); and 3) authority to progress change and respond accordingly (for example, through funding).

It is important to remember that outcomes for children and youth (health, development and wellbeing) also cross policy sectors and therefore the paradigms that must be brokered are not only research-to-policy within a sector, but between sectors. The knowledge broker must consider the best opportunities and methods to facilitate these change processes given the policy environmental context at the time.

Figure 6.1 The knowledge broker sphere of influence

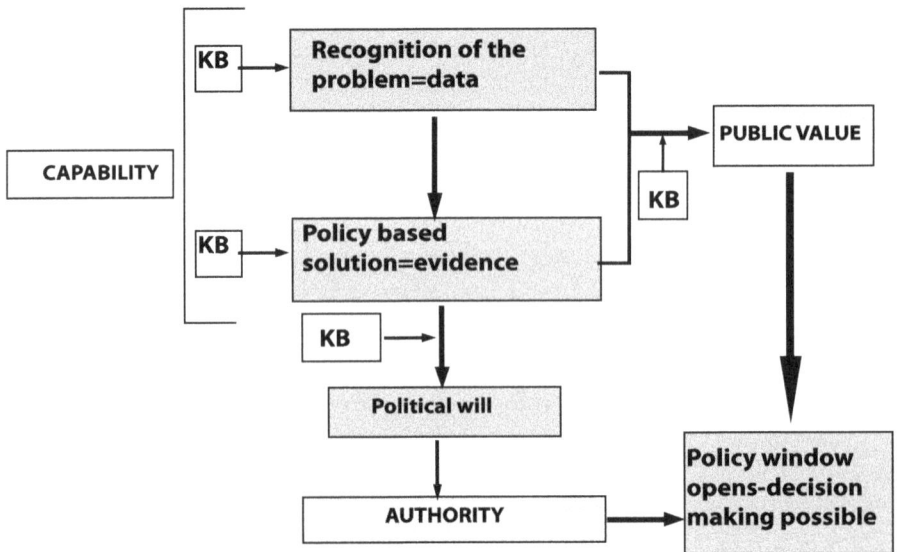

Adapted by Goldfeld from Kingdon (1995) and Moore (2007).

The art and science of knowledge brokering: examples of successful strategies

The knowledge broker can act in a number of differing ways, depending on the opportunities that present themselves. Following are three examples demonstrating where the knowledge broker has played an essential role in helping to achieve an outcome. It is important to note that knowledge-brokering processes are not always heralded or obvious; rather they are often subtle and unnoticed. Knowledge brokers often place leadership in the hands of others, allowing the message to be taken up by those who have authority and the ability to make real change. Knowledge brokering also requires strategic thinking and opportunistic discussions, with an agenda planned well ahead of time.

In each of these examples, the principles outlined by Gladwell are considered in terms of: 1) who are the leaders that need to be engaged as champions and who else can echo this message to others; 2) what is the key message or story that needs to be told—the 'sticky message'; and 3) what are the environmental opportunities? Therefore, for each example, the methodology has varied to make the most of the environmental context. The processes have all been iterative and there has been variable success; however, they hopefully highlight the added value of a knowledge broker in transforming environments and enabling change.

While these examples focus mainly on embedding an evidence-based approach in the policy world, it is similarly important to work with researchers to help craft their ideas and projects within a policy context. It is by understanding the constraints that policymakers work within that opportunities that are often missed can be better realised by researchers and policymakers alike. For example, discussing with policymakers research ideas at an early stage of thinking will ensure that the researcher understands where their work might best be positioned (and whether the research is timely or should perhaps be rethought), and the policymaker already knows that the research they are interested in is under way. It is win-win.

Finally, while each of these examples discusses the specific role of the knowledge broker, it is important to note that none of the work described has been undertaken by the knowledge broker in isolation. For each example there was active recruitment of 'like-minded' colleagues and leaders to be both active change agents (the law of the few) and those who were the transmitters of the message.

Example 1: priority setting for children

Understanding the problems facing children today requires us to start from a public health and prevention approach to child health, development, learning and wellbeing; to recognise the importance of social determinants and an ecological explanatory framework as central to guiding future action; and to consider outcomes that require a focus on early identification and management within this process. Four areas emerge from the literature (National Research Council Institute of Medicine 2000; Ochiltree and Moore 2001).

First, contemporary research now emphasises the importance of the first few years of life on the child's developing brain. Brain development in those early years is very dependent on the quality of the care environment. A secure start makes a difference.

Second, biological and environmental factors in the early years are seen to have consequences in later life—for good and sometimes for ill. Poor literacy skills, early school leaving, aggression, adult mental health problems, violent behaviour, criminality and medical conditions including obesity, diabetes and cardiovascular disease can all be seen to have precursors in early childhood.

Third, a body of evidence is suggesting how early intervention is cost effective. Interventions can significantly alter the developmental pathways of children and improve a range of adult outcomes. There are multiple benefits from such an investment.

Fourth, there is evidence of how improved outcomes can best be gained. Effective interventions recognise the intense commitment of parents, and other primary carers, and support this. They are based on parental and family involvement, community development and local identification of gaps and solutions.

In 2004, the Victorian Government undertook a priority-setting process to determine where it should focus effort in regard to children's outcomes. Reviewing this evidence base was essential if the Victorian Government, and particularly the Department of Human Services,[1] was to know where it should focus its attention—that is, how to invest as wisely as possible when faced with competing choices. In developing policy, there are often competing agendas. The priority-setting approach offers the opportunity to ensure the development of evidence-based policy that focuses on the issues that need to be addressed and for which there are effective interventions (Department of Human Services 2004).

---

1   In 2009, the Department of Human Services split into the Department of Health and the Department of Human Services.

From the knowledge-brokering point of view, this was a vehicle to: 1) raise awareness about the importance of outcomes for children across a range of stakeholders within government, including senior decision makers; 2) integrate an evidence-based approach into priority setting; 3) challenge decision makers to consider what effective interventions were not being implemented, and what ineffective interventions were continuing to be funded; and 4) engage policymakers in a process that focused on evidence and outcomes, rather than outputs and programs.

There were two key roles for the knowledge broker in the process. First, there was a need to work actively with policymakers, using evidence-based priority-setting tools to determine the overall priorities for children (creating the evidence-based messages). A priority-setting methodology was applied to children's outcomes and determinants, with scoring against prevalence, efficacy of intervention, impact and community concern. Two different equations were applied to the scores to produce two alternative lists of priority areas. Once the issues were ranked for each equation, a threshold line was established to delineate the priorities.

In this role, the knowledge broker was able to transfer the scientific evidence into a policy context. Once this was completed, however, there was a risk that the process would stall as a venture without authority (see Figure 6.1). Therefore, although there was a good understanding of the evidence by a number of policymakers, further commitment (the 'tipping point' in policy terms) was unlikely without senior management being able to transmit the message. The risk in this process was that knowledge would be brokered, but there would be no lasting effect. It was at this point that the art of knowledge brokering became most influential and helped facilitate the involvement of the highest levels of management from within government. For sustainability, the process required broader strategic thinking and influence (being the brokering of evidence) to ensure there were leaders to make the final decisions about priorities and convert the 'sticky' messages to action. Knowledge brokering in this context required the recruitment of others (the 'law of the few') to influence senior leaders as to the value of this process in determining priority efforts for children. The outcome was that cross-departmental groups were established to work on four key priorities for children with the imprimatur of the senior executive. In this case example, knowledge brokering assisted the policy and political processes by using data and evidence to recognise the issues for children and articulating policy-based solutions through priority setting. Although the science was necessary to consider evidence within a policy context, the art of knowledge brokering was necessary to ensure that priority action areas for children could continue to be addressed within usual departmental processes and would not be sidelined or ignored.

Example 2: establishing the Victorian Child and Adolescent Monitoring System

It is clear from Figure 6.1 that data capability is an important aspect of successful and sustainable policy processes. It could be argued that without data there is little chance of successful change (or any way of knowing whether outcomes have been achieved). The role of data and information in shaping policy and setting government agendas has never been more critical. In an environment of competing agendas linked to both economic and political outcomes, data have the capacity to significantly alter where decision makers will finally focus attention and commitment as well as ensuring there is a capacity to evaluate the effectiveness of programs where significant funding has been applied. Data should therefore be considered the core of any agenda for children.

This idea has been reinforced nationally (Goldfeld and Oberklaid 2005) and internationally. For example, Rigby et al. (2003), in their paper on the European indicators of child health ('Child Health Indicators of Life Development', or 'CHILD'), noted that data 'should be in the centre of child health and not at the periphery of health monitoring'.

In this example, the knowledge-brokering function was to capitalise on the opportunity that presented itself through the establishment of the Office for Children in the Victorian Department of Human Services in 2005. The office was clearly committed to children's health, development, learning, safety and wellbeing. While the department already monitored a range of child-related outcomes, only limited data were collected on a reasonably universal basis. Although some data were collected by other agencies, including other departments and the Australian Bureau of Statistics, neither departmental nor external sources covered all priority areas, particularly newly emerging issues of concern. Additional ways of collecting data were required. Establishing the Victorian Child and Adolescent Monitoring System (VCAMS) (Department of Education and Early Childhood Development 2007) within the Office for Children[2] was a critical step in ensuring that data would remain central to policy for children in the short and long term and be available for future knowledge-brokering processes. The objectives of VCAMS were to

- build a state-wide integrated monitoring and reporting system that was directly linked to policy and planning activities

- develop continuing data-collection strategies to address data gaps

---

2   The Office for Children merged with the Victorian Department of Education to become the Department of Education and Early Childhood Development in 2007.

- ensure data were available, analysed and utilised for policy, planning, evaluation and research
- report regularly on the health, development, learning, safety and wellbeing of Victoria's children and adolescents.

In helping to establish VCAMS, the knowledge broker played a more traditional brokering role: preparing information for high-level decision makers that would enable them to make evidence-based decisions. Key to this process, however, was ensuring that policymakers at all levels of decision making understood the importance of data and would therefore support any further developments necessary over time and utilise the data for their own policymaking. In parallel with internal influence, external advice was also sought, capitalising on relationships with researchers to ensure that any proposals were based on the best science available. Clearly, having established networks across the research and policy arenas was of major benefit.

Using Gladwell's principles again, the power of context was very important for this process. Although there had been much advocacy for better data collection and monitoring of outcomes in the previous two years, it was only the establishment of the Office for Children—with a direct mandate to report on children's outcomes—that enabled the developmental and conceptual work for VCAMS to be undertaken. Subsequently, all of the objectives of VCAMS have been met to some extent (Cleary et al. 2008), including the development of an outcomes framework (Goldfeld et al. 2007) and two state-wide reports (Hood et al. 2006, 2008).

Example 3: creating data for planning and community development

The knowledge broker can also act to influence change at the local government or community level. This example focuses on research into policy and practice at the local level.

The Australian Early Development Index (AEDI) is a population measure of child development completed by teachers on children in their first year of formal schooling. The AEDI covers the domains of physical, social, emotional, cognitive and language development as well as general communication. The data are collected on all children in a geographic area, thereby providing small area-level data.

The Australian Early Development Index: Building Better Communities for Children project was undertaken in 54 communities throughout Australia, providing results, reports and maps describing how children in each area were developing by the time they reached school age (Centre for Community Child Health and the Telethon Institute of Child Health Research 2007). The project was conducted by the Centre for Community Child Health in partnership with the Telethon Institute for Child Health Research. It was an initiative of the Australian Government's National Agenda for Early Childhood with support from Shell Australia. In 2008, the incoming Rudd Government committed to a national roll-out of the AEDI with continuing funding from the Australian Government. While the story of how the AEDI came to be funded and then grew to the stage of a national roll-out is also a story about knowledge brokering (Goldfeld et al. 2008), the focus of the discussion below is on how knowledge brokering at a local level can have a substantial impact on the uptake and utility of the data at a local level.

Although knowledge brokers have traditionally been considered within the central government and policymaking contexts, the increasing program and policy activity aimed at children in local communities opens an opportunity for locally informed knowledge brokers to take a stronger role. The community-level knowledge brokering and the accompanying need to effect change are in some ways a microcosm of what can be seen at the broader policy level. The local ability to create a tipping point can, however, be far more probable.

For example, through the AEDI data-implementation process, communities must consider how they might change outcomes for children. This requires a knowledge broker to: 1) explain the nature of the data for that community (for example, by holding forums at which the results are properly explained); 2) facilitate the bringing together of stakeholders from various sectors within the community such as cross-sectoral strategy meetings to plan actions as a result of the AEDI; and 3) work with local governments to empower communities to effect change (for example, by advocating for certain evidence-based interventions or policy changes that are likely to result in local improvements). The knowledge broker therefore has to assess the evidence, interpret it for local circumstances and market or communicate the results. In this context, experts (or more centrally based knowledge brokers) can work with local leaders to build local knowledge-brokering capacity.

In once again taking up Gladwell's principles about the importance of messages, the environmental context and leadership, the knowledge broker can act to help communities better understand how to utilise the results of the AEDI (the message) to create change at a local level (context).

There is therefore impetus—at least in this context—to ensure that local knowledge brokers have the full range of skills necessary to galvanise the community, utilise the data evidence and consider how best to synthesise and communicate the research evidence that responds to the data and will most likely result in improved outcomes for local children. In the evaluation of the AEDI, it is clear that the AEDI process itself (as well as the results) has been successful in promoting the emerging concept of the local knowledge broker. In a number of areas, local leaders have emerged to bring stakeholders together to discuss early childhood and have utilised the AEDI to galvanise local action, bring in funds and consider the most effective community responses to the results (Sayers et al. 2007).

Conclusion

In Australia, there are significant areas of concern about children's health and development, with increasing disparities (especially for Indigenous children) and many health issues on the rise (Richardson and Prior 2005). At the same time, there is increasing interest from governments in improving the lives of children. In order to capitalise on the policy environment, however, and influence social change over time for all children, there is a pressing need to build capacity (through the policy and research fields) for knowledge brokering in child health and development. While it is important for researchers to actively engage with policymakers in the development and dissemination of research, knowledge brokering requires more active, sustained and planned effort than discussions or forums. Further, in actively developing more knowledge brokers, we should not underestimate the importance of the art of persuasion and communication in brokering the science of evidence.

References

Bronson, R. C., Rover, C., Ewing, R. and McBride, T. D. 2006, 'Researchers and policymakers: travellers in parallel universes', *American Journal of Preventive Medicine*, vol. 30, no. 2, pp. 164–72.

Canadian Health Services Research Foundation (CHSRF) 2003, *The Theory and Practice of Knowledge Brokering in Canada's Health System*, Canadian Health Services Research Foundation, Ottawa, viewed 3 May 2010, <http://www. chsrf.ca/brokering/pdf/Theory_and_Practice_e.pdf>

Canadian Health Services Research Foundation (CHSRF) 2008, *Glossary of Knowledge Exchange Terms as Used by the Foundation*, Canadian Health Services Research Foundation, Ottawa, viewed 3 May 2010, <http://www. chsrf.ca/keys/glossary_e.php>

Centre for Community Child Health and the Telethon Institute of Child Health Research 2007, *AEDI Community Results 2004–2006 Report*, Centre for Community Child Health and the Telethon Institute of Child Health Research, Subiaco, WA, viewed 3 May 2010, <http://video.wch.org.au/aedi/AustralianCommunitiesApril07.pdf>

Cleary, J., Goldfeld, S., Gabriel, S. and Siemon, D. 2008, 'Information for action: developing the Victorian Child and Adolescent Monitoring System (VCAMS)', *Australasian Epidemiologist*, vol. 15, no. 3 (December), pp. 19–23.

Department of Education and Early Childhood Development 2008, *Victorian Child and Adolescent Monitoring System*, Department of Education and Early Childhood Development, Government of Victoria, Melbourne, viewed 29 September 2008, <http://www.education.vic.gov.au/ocecd/statewide-outcomes.html>

Department of Human Services 2004, *Establishing Priorities for Gain: The health, development, safety and wellbeing of Victoria's Children*, Department of Human Services, Government of Victoria, Melbourne.

Gladwell, M. 2002, *The Tipping Point: How little things can make a big difference*, Little, Brown and Company, New York.

Goldfeld, S. and Oberklaid, F. 2005, 'Maintaining an agenda for children and young people: the key role of data in linking policy, politics and outcomes', *Medical Journal of Australia*, vol. 183, pp. 1–3.

Goldfeld, S., Muth, P. and Siemon, D. 2007, 'The Victorian child and adolescent outcomes framework', *Child Outcomes*, issue 1, Department of Education and Early Childhood Development, Government of Victoria, Melbourne.

Goldfeld, S., Sayers, M., Brinkman, S., Silburn, S. and Oberklaid, F. 2008, 'The process and policy challenges of adapting and implementing the Canadian early development instrument in Australia', *Early Education and Development*, vol. 20, no. 6, pp. 978–91.

Hood, S., Goldfeld, S., Muth, P., Cleary, J., Farooqui, A. and Hayes, L. 2006, *The State of Victoria's Children Report 2006*, Department of Human Services, Government of Victoria, Melbourne.

Hood, S., Lamb, K., Elkington, D., Grant, M. and Apted, H. 2008, *The State of Victoria's Young People*, Department of Education and Early Childhood Development and the Department of Planning and Community Development, Government of Victoria, Melbourne.

Kingdon, J. 1995, *Agendas, Alternatives and Public Policies*, Second edn, Harper Collins College, New York.

Moore, M. 2007, *Creating Public Value: Strategic management in government*, Second edn, Harvard University, Cambridge, Mass.

National Research Council Institute of Medicine 2000, *From Neurons to Neighbourhoods*, National Academy Press, Washington, DC.

Ochiltree, G. and Moore, T. 2001, *Best Start for Children. The evidence base underlying investment in the early years*, Department of Human Services, Government of Victoria, Melbourne.

Richardson, S. and Prior, M. 2005, *No Time to Lose: The well-being of Australia's children*, Melbourne University Press, Vic.

Rigby, M., Kohler, L., Blair, M. and Metchler, R. 2003, 'Child health indicators for Europe: a priority for a caring society', *European Journal of Public Health*, vol. 13, no. 3, pp. 38–46.

Sayers, M., Coutts, M., Goldfeld, S., Oberklaid, F., Brinkman, S. A. and Silburn, S. R. 2007, 'Building better communities for children: community implementation and evaluation of the Australian Early Development Index', *Early Education and Development*, vol. 18, no. 3, pp. 519–34.

Snow, J. 1885, *On the Mode of Communication of Cholera*, John Churchill, London.

7. Creating and implementing large-scale parenting education programs: bridging research, decision making and practice

Linda Neuhauser

Introduction

There is increasing evidence that interventions during pregnancy and early childhood can profoundly affect children's long-term health and wellbeing (Case et al. 2005; Gomby et al. 1995; Heckman 2000; Karoly et al. 1998; McCain and Mustard 2002). For example, parents' knowledge and practices related to health care, bonding with their baby, nutrition, smoking, safety and other factors have a strong influence on children's healthy development (License 2004; NICHD Early Child Care Research Network 2000; Shonkoff and Philips 2000; Shore 1997). Research shows that parenting education is effective, including the more affordable approaches that use mass communication (Neuhauser et al. 2007a). It has been challenging, however, to translate these findings into successful, large-scale and sustainable programs (Green 2001; Simpson 2004; Zervignon-Hakes 1995).

In fact, research translation is an underlying problem of nearly all educational interventions because of the many obstacles to sharing knowledge persuasively across stakeholder groups, systems and settings (Bammer 2005; Bammer and Smithson 2008; Furler 2008; Green and Glasgow 2006; Innvaer et al. 2002; Neuhauser et al. 2007b; Stokols 2006; Sussman et al. 2006; Tsui 2006). The World Health Organisation (WHO 2004) labels this issue the 'know–do gap'. During the past two decades, there has been intense interest in understanding the reasons for the gap and identifying strategies to bridge it. A key finding is that integrating science for action requires the active involvement of researchers, practitioners and decision makers (Clark and Kelly 2005; Kerner et al. 2005; Lavis et al. 2003; Leischow et al. 2008; Stokols et al. 2008; Tsui 2006; van Kammen et al. 2005, 2006; Zervignon-Hakes 1995). For example, in their systematic review of effective innovations, Greenhalgh et al. (2004) conclude that interpersonal networks among stakeholders are necessary to diffuse knowledge. Or, as Lomas (2007:130) comments: 'Human interaction is the engine that drives research into practice.'

The focus on social factors that promote research translation is a notable departure from the traditional technical view of research as a 'product' to be adopted by decision makers and automatically applied by practitioners (Lomas 2000). Studies suggest that a more effective model is one in which stakeholder groups use 'multiple interacting processes' to build consensus around a course of action (Walshe and Rundall 2001)—such as a parenting education program—and work together on its implementation and evaluation. It has been difficult, however, to move researchers, decision makers and practitioners from their historically separate roles into close collaboration (WHO 2004). For this reason, there is increased interest in the value of 'knowledge brokers' and supporting institutions to link these stakeholder groups.

This chapter provides an overview of knowledge brokering and how it was critical to developing, testing and extending a parenting education program to benefit more than 500 000 families each year. The specific objectives of this chapter are to: 1) discuss issues related to brokering knowledge among researchers, decision makers and practitioners; 2) present a case study of knowledge brokering among these stakeholders to develop a large-scale parenting education program; and 3) suggest strategies to improve knowledge brokering among stakeholders.

Knowledge brokering definitions

'Knowledge brokering' and 'knowledge sharing' are related to other terms in common use. Tsui (2006:5) defines *knowledge sharing* as 'the process of exchanging knowledge (skills, experience, and understanding [and I would add: evidence]) among researchers, policymakers, and service providers'. *Knowledge brokering* implies the added dynamic dimensions of influence and negotiation. *Research 'translation'* is an extended process describing how research knowledge that is directly or indirectly relevant to health or wellbeing eventually serves the public (adapted from Sussman et al. 2006). Although 'translational research' is sometimes assumed to be a linear process from research to its application, Stokols (2006) describes it as a loop that circulates continuously between research and its application and revision, across multiple actors, sectors and settings.

Dissemination and *research dissemination* are other common terms that can refer to 'an active and strategically planned process whereby new or existing knowledge, interventions, or practices are spread' (Kiefer et al. 2005:14). King et al. (1998:237) describe dissemination as part of the cycle translating research into action and emphasise that it can be viewed as a 'two-way process that exchanges knowledge between researcher and implementer groups'. *Knowledge integration* is also a contemporary term for knowledge that is viewed as tightly woven within priorities, culture and contexts (Bammer 2005; Best et al. 2007). In such 'systems perspectives', relationships at all levels are keys to access and to integrate knowledge for decision making. Bammer (2005) and Gibson (2003) support the view that interactions between researchers, policymakers and implementers need to go beyond the idea of *knowledge exchange* and influence to 'transform' knowledge so that is invested with meaning and power that binds parties to new thinking and action.

In this chapter, I use 'knowledge brokering' to reflect a more comprehensive meaning of the above terms: 'a cyclical interaction of stakeholders to integrate and transform their experiences and evidence across time and place in pursuit of a common goal.'

Challenges to brokering knowledge

Increasingly, we are learning about key barriers to knowledge brokering. Bammer (2005), Lomas (2000, 2007), Kerner et al. (2005), King et al. (1998), Leischow et al. (2008), Tsui (2006) and others point out the differing incentives and systems in which researchers, decision makers and practitioners operate. Researchers, for example, are motivated more to conduct basic, rather than applied studies and to communicate results via academic journals—a lengthy process and one that often restricts information for other stakeholders. Conversely, decision makers often need timely, well-digested information to make decisions that fit within yearly budgets or political terms. Practitioners might prefer to draw on their own experiences and might have inadequate access to understandable research findings or limited power to change practices within their institutions. For all parties, knowledge sharing requires additional time, funding, sensitivity and persistence to work across these diverse cultures. Given such obstacles, it is not surprising that the aforementioned scholars also point out that stakeholder groups often lack the strong relationships and participatory processes that are at the heart of successful knowledge brokering.

Leveraging theoretical guidance and empirical evidence

Many disciplines offer conceptual guidance to improve knowledge brokering. For example, social ecology (Stokols 2000) and systems models (Lenaway et al. 2006) emphasise the interdependence among sectors and settings and their mutual influence. Participatory/action research frameworks (Israel et al. 1998; Minkler and Wallerstein 2003) suggest processes to link stakeholders and organisations for better research and application. Diffusion of innovations (Greenhalgh et al. 2004; Rogers 1982) and other communication models (Neuhauser and Kreps 2003) describe phases of change as knowledge is integrated into action. There are newer models that link multiple frameworks, such as Bammer's (2005) integration and implementation science model and Stokols' (2006) trans-disciplinary action research.

Little empirical evidence exists about the effectiveness of specific knowledge-brokering processes (Abrams 2006; Kerner et al. 2005; Tsui 2006). Observations of collaborative work across sectors and disciplines, however, suggest a number of potentially important factors, including (Bammer 2005; Bielak et al. 2008; Ferlie et al. 2000; Greenhalgh et al. 2004; Hutchings et al. 2006; Lomas 2000, 2007; Sussman et al. 2006; van Kammen et al. 2005; WHO 2004)

- leadership and negotiation skills to work across sectors
- multi-institutional support for collaborative work
- strong participatory processes
- respect for others' models and methods
- development of a common language
- regular face-to-face meetings
- verbal and non-verbal communication skills
- motivation and incentives to participate
- expertise in problem-based research and practice
- adequate funding and time.

Among the most innovative and promising efforts are those that explicitly train knowledge brokers and create systems to support their work. For example, the Canadian Health Services Research Foundation (2003) defines its role as a 'knowledge-brokering agency'. It trains health researchers in knowledge-brokering skills, requires that each research project has a decision maker as a co-investigator and that practitioners who are to implement research results co-produce research summaries. The Netherlands Organization for Health Research and Development (ZonMw) pioneers knowledge transfer by organising meetings between researchers, practitioners and decision makers, gathering information about innovation processes and by assigning an 'implementation advisor' to each research program (van Kammen et al. 2005).

Clearly, knowledge brokering is critical to foster successful collaboration between researchers, practitioners and decision makers, which is needed for better societal interventions. How might we apply what has been learned about knowledge brokering to improve parenting education? Below, I describe the knowledge-brokering strategies used in a large-scale program in the United States.

Knowledge brokering in the First 5 California program

In 1998, the residents of the US state of California approved a tobacco tax to establish a commission that would support programs to benefit young children and their parents. The resulting First 5 California Children and Families Commission ('First 5'; <http://www.ccfc.ca.gov/>) decided to create a Kit for New Parents that would be distributed free of charge to approximately 500 000 expectant and new parents every year. This ambitious effort required designing a kit that would be low cost and include key evidenced-based information about pregnancy and caring for young children, and linkages to important health, parenting, social and other services state-wide. The kit had to be engaging and easy to use for diverse parents and practical for service providers to distribute. It also needed to be accepted by policymakers and service providers in each of the state's 58 counties (each with its own local government and health and social systems). Finally, to determine whether the kit initiative would be approved as a long-term investment, policymakers would need evidence of the kit's positive impact on parents and providers.

During 2000, a multimedia, low-cost (US$17.50), low-literacy kit was designed and tested with the input of researchers, service providers, parents and state policymakers. Our research group at the Health Research for Action Center at the University of California, Berkeley, conducted pilot and longitudinal studies with parents and providers state-wide. In 2001, the kit was formally launched and distributed through the state's 58 counties according to local plans. It is now available to most new parents each year (about 500 000) and their service providers through prenatal programs, delivery hospitals, nurse home visits, telephone hotlines and other means. The evaluations showed that the kit significantly increased parents' knowledge and positive practices and was a valuable resource for providers. In 2004, First 5 decided to approve the kit as a long-term investment. Neuhauser and colleagues (2007a) report on the kit's development and evaluation.

The process to develop, implement and evaluate the kit and determine its long-term support posed many knowledge-brokering challenges. The next section describes strategies that facilitated this work among stakeholders.

Six strategies to broker knowledge

1. Identify effective 'knowledge brokers' to lead and inspire stakeholders

Rob Reiner, a well-known US film director and advocate for children, created the tobacco tax measure that established First 5, chaired the First 5 Commission, proposed the kit initiative and was the primary 'knowledge broker' for this effort. Reiner brought multiple strengths to the knowledge-broker role. He leveraged his worldwide celebrity, his credibility and experience on behalf of children's issues and his legislative savvy.

In the 1990s, Reiner established the international I Am Your Child foundation to highlight early childhood issues and strategies to address them. He helped organise a White House conference on early childhood issues hosted by President Bill Clinton and created television specials on this topic. He then established the Parents Action for Children initiative to provide education and support for the 65 million US parents. For each of these efforts, Reiner was successful in identifying advisors and supporters, including the small number of staff working at his non-profit organisations.

Reiner's brokering skills were equally effective in the legislative arena, where he led the passage of the proposition that authorised First 5. His approach was to organise his colleagues in media, early childhood and other sectors to gain state-wide support for the initiative. His media skills and recognition as being knowledgeable and passionate about early childhood issues were a powerful combination.

When he became chairman of First 5, Reiner used his reputation and charisma to develop good relationships with legislators, other policymakers, leaders from major service provider groups and researchers from universities and think tanks working on children's issues. He was able to interpret 'knowledge' and communicate it to stakeholders in a way that related to their own concerns and motivations. He also had the gift of communicating and 'transforming' knowledge about the initiative so that it inspired stakeholders' enthusiastic commitment. After he had secured the approval of the First 5 Commission to develop the kit and have an initial pilot test, he worked to engage and help local policymakers and service providers take on local leadership. Stakeholders from

California's 58 counties were invited to attend state-level First 5 Commission meetings and to present and debate ideas about the program—an approach that sparked excitement and helped create effective plans.

2. Use participatory approaches from the start

From the outset, First 5 used highly participatory processes to design, test, revise and make decisions about the kit program. During the design phase, materials were reviewed and tested with parents, providers, health experts, representatives of advocacy groups and state policymakers. This process identified a number of initial errors that were corrected before the state-wide launch. Similarly, a participatory process was set up to design and refine kit distribution. First 5 established decentralised governance in each of the 58 counties that was designed to link policymakers, service providers and parents who would define local distribution plans.

As mentioned in strategy number one, researchers were engaged at the state level to advise on evidence-based information to include in the kit and to evaluate kit impacts. Counties were also encouraged to work with researchers to conduct local evaluations to help refine local plans. The close linkage of researchers, service providers and policymakers at state and local levels greatly helped share knowledge about the kit development, implementation and evaluation. It also helped stakeholders openly discuss and resolve issues about the kit. For example, when research results showed that the kit was more effective when given out before the baby's birth, many counties took that into consideration in their distribution plans. Likewise, service providers were encouraged to share issues and ideas at county, regional and state-wide meetings attended by First 5 policymakers. Stakeholders in remote areas, who could not attend these meetings, communicated their views through evaluators who interviewed them. Over the years, these participatory processes among stakeholders have become a strong 'feedback loop' to continuously identify problems and improvements.

3. Identify and address stakeholder needs, commitments and barriers

When the First 5 Commission initially approved the program, there were many concerns from stakeholders in local counties about whether the kit would be effective and whether systems could be set up to distribute it. For example, some researchers and service providers thought that, from their experience or interpretation of the literature, Spanish-speaking parents and those with limited literacy would not likely benefit from the kit. Policymakers and service providers worried about whether large-scale distributions would overwhelm systems and divert energy from other important activities. These concerns were discussed at the state First 5 meetings where stakeholders engaged in solving problems. As evidence from the pilot evaluation became available, researchers communicated it to other stakeholders. During the first six months of the pilot evaluation, results showed that Spanish speakers had excellent outcomes from using the kit, as did lower-educated parents. As principal investigator of the study, I presented findings at the state-wide meetings, had them put on the First 5 web site and made presentations in local counties to decision makers and key service providers. The evaluation was also designed to elicit the views of policymakers and key service providers in each of the 58 counties. The findings were 'brokered' to influence First 5 to make needed changes in the initiative—such as making the kits smaller so that they would be easier to store and distribute and developing kits in Asian languages.

4. Emphasise effective communication

As in all knowledge-brokering situations, communication played a central role in integrating stakeholder ideas for the kit program. As mentioned earlier, it helped that Reiner was a 'master communicator' and got this initiative off to a very positive and exciting start. Once the pilot initiative was under way and counties had to grapple with devising local plans and making the kit program successful, communication remained a critical knowledge-brokering strategy. For example, policymakers and service providers often have limited access to research results that they can understand and apply (Cheng et al. 2008; Clark and Kelly 2005). To overcome this problem, our research group worked with public relations firms to extract one and two-page summaries of key evaluation results and recommendations for specific ways findings could be used to improve the kit program. We also worked with a firm that specialised in creating engaging, easy to understand 'graphic reports' to produce a 15-page executive summary (in print and online) for researchers, policymakers and practitioners. In addition, we had the usual scientific technical reports and publications for researchers to review.

Oral presentations were also a challenge, given the diverse stakeholders. First 5 developed a system of having very brief presentations at its state-wide meetings with ample time for visiting stakeholders to comment. The content of the presentations was extracted into short written summaries that were handed out at the meetings and put online. Because the chairman of First 5 was a film director, short videos of the impact of the kit's use among parents and providers became one popular way to broker knowledge in a visual, emotional way.

5. Share and celebrate achievements and benefits to all stakeholders

Stakeholders have different roles in designing, implementing and evaluating programs and sometimes this prevents their seeing the 'big-picture' value of their efforts. Policymakers approve programs, but might not grasp how activities work in the field and what they mean to beneficiaries. Researchers analyse program effects, but might not feel that they can take any credit for a program they did not implement. Practitioners are often caught up in the details of everyday implementation and might not understand the impact of their work.

Through its intensive emphasis on participatory processes, First 5 was effective in linking stakeholders in the work and helping them understand its impact. For example, when the kit pilot test proved successful, and First 5 decided to launch the kit program state-wide, there was a major event in Hollywood to which the media and stakeholders were invited. The event—hosted by Reiner—took place at a childcare centre that would distribute the kit and included celebrities, local service providers, policymakers and researchers. The event brought out the contributions of each of the stakeholder groups and their value to making the program a success. Periodically, other media events, including those on television and radio, have been held to celebrate milestones of the program. Program impacts are also shared at state and local meetings and on the Internet.

6. Broker knowledge to extend programs

Even if knowledge is brokered effectively and an initiative is successful, it is usually challenging to share that understanding with stakeholders in other settings. After the kit program showed good evidence of positive outcomes (Neuhauser et al. 2007a), there were a number of efforts to engage stakeholders beyond California. The approach began with policymakers in other states and in national and state advocacy organisations for children and parents. Reiner spoke with state governors and brought others involved in the Californian program to explain its operations and outcomes. I attended some of those meetings to present research findings. As in the First 5 program, there was strong emphasis on using communication that would inspire policymakers and other potential stakeholders.

To date, five other US states have begun or completed kit initiatives for all their new parents. Each of these efforts has involved sharing knowledge to help states develop an approach that is adapted to their own needs. For example, when the Virginia G. Piper Trust—a foundation in the state of Arizona—expressed interest in creating a kit program for that state's parents, First 5 stakeholders communicated with them by e-mail (and eventually in person) to describe approaches that had worked in California and problems to avoid. Designers of kit materials—including the publication group at our Health Research for Action Center—helped Arizona colleagues customise one resource for their kit and our research group provided data to Arizona decision makers about the outcomes in our state. Arizona adopted a participatory design process similar to that used in California: the foundation engaged service providers to work with other providers and with parents to draft and test kit materials. The foundation conducted a pilot evaluation of their kit leveraging survey design elements and instruments from the Californian study. Based on the positive outcomes in Arizona, the foundation decision makers have approved long-term funding for their kit program. They are now helping broker their experiences with colleagues in other states.

Conclusions

All too often, knowledge brokering is overlooked as a specific, critical factor in program design, implementation and evaluation (Bammer 2005; Canadian Health Services Research Foundation 2003; Clark and Kelly 2005; Gibson 2003; Greenhalgh et al. 2004; Kerner et al. 2005; Kiefer et al. 2005; Lomas 2000, 2007; van Kammen et al. 2005, 2006; WHO 2004). During the past two decades, theoretical guidance and empirical evidence have provided a good foundation to understand the value of knowledge brokering and the 'lessons learned' to do it well. What we have learned is that knowledge brokers need a range of specific skills and organisational structures to support their work. Initial results of such efforts are promising, especially when there is funding, dedicated efforts to train these 'boundary spanners' and established ways to link them with researchers, decision makers and practitioners.

Knowledge brokering is a revolutionary strategy that can advance the transition from historically weak approaches to powerful ways of creating synergy among researchers, decision makers and practitioners to benefit society. One of the most effective ways to leverage knowledge brokering is to promote interventions that support parents of young children. In the case study presented here, the six knowledge-brokering skills were key in designing, implementing, evaluating and revising a large-scale parenting program that has positively impacted millions of families.

References

Abrams, D. B. 2006, 'Applying transdisciplinary research strategies to understanding and eliminating health disparities', *Health Education and Behavior*, vol. 33, no. 4, pp. 515–31.

Bammer, G. 2005, 'Integration and implementation sciences: building a new specialization', *Ecology and Society*, vol. 10, no. 2, viewed 19 March 2007, <http://www.ecologyandsociety.org/vol10/iss2/art6/>

Bammer, G. and Smithson, M. (eds) 2008, *Uncertainty and Risk: Multidisciplinary perspectives*, Earthscan, London and Sterling, Va.

Best, A., Hiatt, R. A. and Norman, C. D. 2007, 'Knowledge integration: conceptualizing communications in cancer control systems', *Patient Education and Counseling*, vol. 71, no. 3, pp. 319–27.

Bielak, A. T., Campbell, A., Pope, S., Schaefer, K. and Shaxson, L. 2008, 'From science communication to knowledge brokering: the shift from "science push" to "policy pull"', in D. Cheng, M. Claessens, T. Gascoigne, J. Metcalfe, B. Schiele and S. Shi (eds), *Communicating Science in Social Contexts*, Springer Netherlands, The Netherlands.

Canadian Health Services Research Foundation 2003, *The Theory and Practice of Knowledge Brokering in Canada's Health System*, Canadian Health Services Research Foundation, Ottawa, viewed 3 May 2010, <www.chsrf.ca/brokering/pdf/Theory_and_Practice_e.pdf>

Case, A., Fertig, A. and Paxson, C. 2005, 'The lasting impact of childhood health and circumstance', *Journal of Health Economics*, vol. 24, pp. 365–89.

Cheng, D., Claessens, M., Gascoigne, T., Metcalfe, J., Schiele, B. and Shi, S. (eds) 2008, *Communicating Science in Social Contexts*, Springer Netherlands, The Netherlands.

Clark, G. and Kelly, E. 2005, *New Directions for Knowledge Transfer and Knowledge Brokerage in Scotland*, Office of the Chief Researcher, Scottish Executive, Edinburgh, viewed 3 May 2010, <www.scotland.gov.uk/Resource/Doc/69582/0018002.pdf>

Ferlie, E., Fitzgerald, L. and Wood, M. 2000, 'Getting evidence into clinical practice: an organizational behaviour perspective', *Journal of Health Service Research Policy*, vol. 5, pp. 96–102.

Furler, L. 2008, 'Smoke and mirrors: managing uncertainty in the public health sector', in G. Bammer and M. Smithson (eds), *Uncertainty and Risk: Multidisciplinary perspectives*, Earthscan, London and Sterling, Va, pp. 183–93.

Gibson, B. 2003, From transfer to transformation: rethinking the relationship between research and policy, Dissertation, National Centre for Epidemiology and Population Health, The Australian National University, Canberra, viewed 3 May 2010, <http://thesis.anu.edu.au/public/adt-ANU20040528.165124/index.html>

Gomby, D. S., Larner, M. B., Stevenson, C. S., Lewit, E. M. and Behrman, R. E. 1995, 'Long-term outcomes of early childhood programs: analysis and recommendations', *Future Child*, vol. 5, pp. 6–24.

Green, L. W. 2001, 'From research to best practices in other settings and populations', *American Journal of Health Behavior*, vol. 25, pp. 165–78.

Green, L. W. and Glasgow, R. E. 2006, 'Evaluating the relevance, generalization, and applicability of research: issues in external validation and translation methodology', *Evaluation and the Health Professions*, vol. 29, no. 1, pp. 126–53.

Greenhalgh, T., Robert, G., Macfarlane, F., Bate, P. and Kyriakidou, O. 2004, 'Diffusion of innovations in service organizations: systematic review and recommendations', *Milbank Quarterly*, vol. 82, pp. 581–629.

Heckman, J. 2000, *Policies to Foster Human Capital*, Irving B. Harris Graduate School of Public Policy Studies, University of Chicago, Ill.

Hutchings, A., Raine, R., Sanderson, S. and Black, N. 2006, 'A comparison of formal consensus methods used for developing clinical guidelines', *Journal of Health Service Research Policy*, vol. 11, pp. 218–24.

Innvaer, S., Vist, G., Trommald, M. and Oxman, A. 2002, 'Health policy-makers' perceptions of their use of evidence: a systematic review', *Journal of Health Service Research Policy*, vol. 7, pp. 239–44.

Israel, B., Schulz, A., Parker, E. and Becker, A. 1998, 'Review of community-based research: assessing partnership approaches to improve health', *Annual Review of Public Health*, vol. 19, pp. 173–202.

Karoly, L. A., Greenwood, P. W., Everingham, S. S., Hoube, J., Kilburn, M. R., Rydell, C. P., Sanders, M. and Chiesa J. 1998, *Investing in our children: what we know and don't know about the costs and benefits of early childhood interventions*, Report no. MR-898-TCWF, RAND, Santa Monica, Calif.

Kerner, J., Rimer, B. and Emmons, K. 2005, 'Dissemination research and research dissemination: how can we close the gap?', *Health Psychology*, 24, pp. 443–6.

Kiefer, L., Frank, J., Di Ruggerio, E., Dobbins, M., Manuel, D., Gully, P. and Mowat, D. 2005, 'Fostering evidence-based decision-making in Canada: examining the need for a Canadian population and public health evidence centre and research network', *Canadian Journal of Public Health*, vol. 96, pp. I1–19.

King, L., Hawe, P. and Wise, M. 1998, 'Making dissemination a two-way process', *Health Promotion International*, vol. 13, no. 3, pp. 237–44.

Lavis, J. N., Robertson, D., Woodside, J. M., McLeod, C. B. and Abelson, J. 2003, 'Knowledge transfer study group. How can research organizations more effectively transfer research knowledge to decision makers?', *Milbank Quarterly*, vol. 81, pp. 221–48.

Leischow, S. J., Best, A., Trochim, W. M., Clark, P. I., Gallagher, R. S., Marcus, S. E. and Matthews, E. 2008, 'Systems thinking to improve the public's health', *American Journal of Preventive Medicine*, vol. 35, no. 2S, pp. S196–203.

Lenaway, D., Halverson, P., Sotnikov, S., Tilson, H., Corso, L. and Millington, W. 2006, 'Public health systems research: setting a national agenda', *American Journal of Public Health*, vol. 96, no. 3, pp. 410–13.

License, K. 2004, 'Promoting and protecting the health of children and young people', *Child Care Health Development*, vol. 30, pp. 623–35.

Lomas, J. 2000, 'Using "linkage and exchange" to move research into policy at a Canadian foundation', *Health Affairs*, vol. 19, pp. 236–40.

Lomas, J. 2007, 'The in-between world of knowledge brokering', *British Medical Journal*, vol. 334, pp. 129–32.

McCain, M. N. and Mustard, J. F. 2002, *The Early Years Study. Three years later*, Publications Ontario, Toronto.

Minkler, M. and Wallerstein, N. (eds) 2003, *Community Based Participatory Research in Health*, Jossey-Bass, San Francisco.

National Institute of Child Health and Human Development (NICHD) Early Child Care Research Network 2000, 'The relation of child care to cognitive and language development', *Child Development*, vol. 71, pp. 960–80.

Neuhauser, L. and Kreps, G. 2003, 'Rethinking communication in the e-health era', *Journal of Health Psychology*, vol. 8, no. 1, pp. 7–23.

Neuhauser, L., Constantine, W. L., Constantine, N. A., Sokal-Gutierrez, K., Obarski, S. K., Clayton, L., Desai, M., Sumner, G. and Syme, S. L. 2007a, 'Promoting prenatal and early childhood health: evaluation of a statewide materials-based intervention for parents', *American Journal of Public Health*, vol. 97, no. 10, pp. 813–19.

Neuhauser, L., Richardson, D., MacKenzie S. and Minkler, M. 2007b, 'Transdisciplinary and translational doctoral education in public health: issues, trends and innovative models', *Journal of Research Practice*, vol. 3, no. 2, <http://jrp.icaap.org/index.php/jrp/article/view/103/97>

Rogers, E. 1982, *Diffusion of Innovations*, Third edn, Free Press, New York.

Shonkoff, J. P. and Phillips, D. A. (eds) 2000, *From Neurons to Neighborhoods: The science of early child development*, National Academy Press, Washington, DC.

Shore, R. 1997, *Rethinking the Brain: New insights into early development*, Families and Work Institute, New York.

Simpson, L. 2004, 'Lost in translation? Reflections on the role of research in improving health care for children', *Health Affairs*, vol. 23, pp. 125–30.

Stokols, D. 2000, 'Social ecology and behavioral medicine: implications for training, practice, and policy', *Behavioral Medicine*, vol. 26, pp. 129–38.

Stokols, D. 2006, 'Toward a science of transdisciplinary research', *American Journal of Community Psychology*, vol. 38, pp. 63–77.

Stokols, D., Hall, K. L., Taylor, B. K., Moser, R. P. and Syme, S. L. (eds) 2008, 'The science team science: assessing the value of transdisciplinary research', *American Journal of Preventive Medicine*, vol. 35, no. 2S (August).

Sussman, S., Valente, T. W., Rohrbach, L. A., Skara, S. and Pentz M. A. 2006, 'Translation in the health professions: converting science into action', *Evaluation and the Health Professions*, vol. 29, no. 1, pp. 7–32.

Tsui, L. 2006, *A Handbook on Knowledge Sharing: Strategies and recommendations for researchers, policymakers, and service providers*, Community–University Partnership for the Study of Children, Youth, and Families, Alberta.

van Kammen, J., Jansen, K. and Hoeksema, J. 2005, 'Knowledge brokering: a business model', *Italian Journal of Public Health*, vol. 2, p. 120.

van Kammen, J., de Savigny, D. and Sewankambo, H. 2006, 'Using knowledge brokering to promote evidence-based policy-making: the need for support structures', *Bulletin of the World Health Organization*, vol. 84, pp. 608–12.

Walshe, K. and Rundall, T. G. 2001, 'Evidence-based management: from theory to practice in health care', *Milbank Quarterly*, vol. 79, pp. 429–57.

World Health Organisation (WHO) 2004, *World Report on Knowledge for Better Health*, World Health Organisation, Geneva, <www.who.int/rpc/wr2004>

Zervignon-Hakes, A. M. 1995, 'Translating research findings into large-scale public programs and policy', *Future Child*, vol. 5, no. 3.

Future considerations

8. From knowledge transfer to knowledge sharing? Towards better links between research, policy and practice

Brian Head

Introduction

Why is there such a wave of interest in the processes of knowledge transfer, knowledge translation and knowledge brokering? What social and organisational problems seem to require these processes? We all believe that better knowledge, wider understanding and enhanced cooperation will generally lead to better outcomes. Achieving these broad objectives is, however, difficult. In the modern world, we suffer from the dilemma of being information rich and time poor. We are often aware that others have important insights to complement our own perspectives, but the transaction costs of access and engagement are often so high that more cooperative approaches to knowledge and action are doomed to failure. How, then, can we find economical and effective ways to broaden our knowledge and improve our capacity for joint action to tackle major issues?

One common approach is to promote the 'transfer' or 'transmission' of knowledge from one group or sector to others. This is what I call a *knowledge-transmission* approach. The language of 'knowledge transmission' can, however, sometimes imply that some people (experts) have access to important truths that need to be learned, accepted, adopted and implemented by others. Indeed, there are numerous situations where a didactic approach is highly appropriate and efficient. A single authoritative framework is useful and even essential for training and guidance activities where precision and consistency are the top priorities. Examples include the standard operating procedures required to undertake a financial audit; to operate technical equipment; to ensure quality control on a pharmaceutical production line; or to administer clinical procedures such as immunisation. The knowledge generated by scientific expertise is not, however, always simple, readily codified and transferable in this way. Hence the knowledge-transmission model needs to be expanded.

First, expertise tends to grow around disciplinary cultures and professional organisations with their own specialised languages and conceptual frameworks. It is difficult for most people to understand a wide span of disciplinary and professional knowledge, which sometimes has competing as well as complementary approaches to similar issues. *Knowledge translation* is the activity of working to increase understanding across disciplines or professional boundaries. Here, the insights of one group are elucidated and packaged for other audiences.

Second, scientific-technical expertise cannot guarantee general consensus about how problems should be defined and resolved. Thus, there is disagreement on the nature of the problems, the development of preferred solutions and how practical interventions can be effectively implemented. *Knowledge brokering* focuses on harnessing the diverse insights of the professions and academic disciplines around key problems of understanding and action. This approach is by no means straightforward, for reasons outlined below.

Fragmentation and complexity

In the real world, the understanding of issues and problems can often be hotly contested, with a divergence of viewpoints and recommended pathways. This usually arises for two main reasons. The first is the *fragmentation of perspectives* and social understandings, associated with competing value preferences, different occupations, social roles, organisational contexts and knowledge disciplines. The second reason is the inherently *complex* and multi-layered nature of many important problems that attract our attention. Many of these problems arise from multiple causes and are interconnected. For example, there is no simple cause and thus no simple remedy for low educational achievement, child poverty, preventable diseases and addictions, Indigenous disadvantage, ecological degradation, and so on. Hence, as a result of these two factors— fragmentation and complexity—an inclusive and connected approach to knowledge and action is required. It is useful to begin by recognising the different foundations of relevant knowledge.

The *scientific-technical* approach to producing systematic knowledge (with its rigorous protocols for data collection, data quality and testing of causal explanations) provides enormously valuable explanations and insights. Indeed, there could be several relevant disciplinary streams contributing to the scientific knowledge base of a problem. For example, research into drugs and alcohol has benefited from the contributions of criminology, economics, sociology, public health, psychology and neurobiological sciences. Scientific-technical knowledge is, however, only one contributor to the 'knowledge' segment of the knowledge–policy–practice relationship. Sole reliance on rigorous scientific knowledge is impractical, especially since some approaches (for example, the experimental sciences and data modelling) are somewhat disconnected from the 'real world' of professional practice and policy development.

Thus, in addition to scientific-technical knowledge, other important knowledge contributions arise from the *professionals and practitioners* who manage programs, deliver services and assist clients. This realm of 'practice' knowledge is rich, diverse and enlivened by the practitioners' familiarity with numerous cases, clients and contexts. Practitioner knowledge, at its best, is alive to situational experience (McAdam et al. 2007; Schon 1983; Wenger 1998), but develops in professional silos. The world of 'practice wisdom', shared and communicated among practitioners, is not typically characterised by field trials and rigorous testing of data quality. Nevertheless, there are many pressures, especially in contemporary health and social care programs, for practitioners to follow 'best-practice' codes and procedures, shaped by the need for professional accountability and informed by the findings of scientific research on the efficacy of various approaches (Mullen et al. 2008).

The third realm of relevant knowledge is *policy* development and its link to political accountability—the realm of politicians and senior public servants. Policymakers do not simply follow and *adopt* the findings of scientific research and professional practice. Rather, policymakers *make use of* a wide range of information and ideas, as part of their broad consideration of arguments for and against policy adjustment, options for the balancing of interests and calculations about support and legitimacy (Bowen and Zwi 2005; Head 2008a).

A fourth realm of relevant knowledge is the direct experience of citizens who are *users of services*—for example, stakeholders involved as clients, carers or advocates in local community organisations. Their views can easily be neglected or overlooked, unless given formal weight through the consultation and evaluation processes of a program review or publicised through advocacy activities in the media.

The rise of collaborative networks

Research, policy and practice tend to operate with different concerns, languages and time lines (Brownson et al. 2006; Lomas 1990; Shonkoff 2000). In this sense, knowledge is 'sticky' and contextual and few individuals have the skills and time to 'translate' knowledge across these disciplinary and organisational divides.

In a number of areas of human development and human services, professionals and informed stakeholders have concluded that complex issues of wellbeing are not amenable to technical solutions by a set of experts. These big issues can best be tackled by collective efforts in which representatives of research, policy and practice pool their scientific and practical knowledge about what needs to be done. Accordingly, collaborative networks (such as those funded in recent years by the Australian Research Council) have developed forums to facilitate dialogue and consensus between researchers, policymakers and practitioners about research priorities and the implications of research findings for more effective interventions (Head and Stanley 2007). The emphasis is less on basic research (that is, identifying and filling 'gaps' in knowledge) and more on mobilising the best available applied knowledge, drawn from various sectors.

The network approach has identified the need for much improved interaction and communication across the policy, practice and research sectors. For example, how can the fruits of applied research be disseminated in more accessible forms that can be understood and utilised by policymakers and practitioners (Feldman and Kane 2003; Lewig et al. 2006)? Equally, how can the *tacit* knowledge of practitioners be made explicit and shared more widely (McAdam et al. 2007)? In other words, how can the insights of 'practice wisdom' be collated and communicated to inform the work of researchers and policymakers (Salveron et al. 2006; Schorr 2003)? In fact, the communication of knowledge needs to be multi-directional, so that all sectors are better informed about the specific needs and approaches of the others. This allows for mutual understanding and mutual adjustment. Collaborative networks have the objective of knowledge sharing across sectors and disciplines as a basis for more effective policy frameworks and service systems. The question then becomes: what are the most effective approaches to better interaction and mutual understanding?

Although there could be a shared desire to address program/service improvement, the problem of professional silos and fragmentation of knowledge leads to a dispersion of uncoordinated effort. It follows that strategies are needed for promoting interaction between individuals from all relevant sectors. The initial purposes of such interaction are to improve flows of information, improve mutual understanding and thus improve relationships and trust. Production and circulation of documentation are important for mutual understanding, further analysis and for advocacy purposes. Documents alone, however, are insufficient; face-to-face contact seems to be the best way to ensure that relevant insights and knowledge are provided to those who need them in each sector (Lomas 2000).

From interaction to strategic change

Given the entrenched difficulties associated with the establishment of knowledge sharing and brokering across sectors and disciplines, many different activities and techniques are being pursued to promote useful interaction and sharing of ideas (Tsui 2006). These might be understood as ranging in intensity from casual interaction through to regular structured dialogue and engagement around major projects. As informal networks of interaction are developed, a potential basis is built for cooperative activities into the future. Networks can give rise to cross-sectoral teams focusing on specific needs and challenges, perhaps in a local area. Interest networks on particular topics can be established with participation from all sectors. These could operate at a local, regional or even national scale depending on access to communications technology. Networks of interaction are useful and necessary, but more fundamental types of behavioural change are also necessary within each sector to bridge the disciplines and accelerate strategic actions across the sectors to tackle major social problems.

Some challenges and issues for policymakers, researchers and practitioners are briefly noted below.

For policymakers, the key questions might include

- are we working on the most important problems (have we taken account of the views of clients and professional service providers, as well as our political leaders)

- are we seeking to expand the 'space' available inside public agencies to learn, reflect and develop new approaches

- are we seeking to involve practitioners more deeply in the design, delivery and evaluation of programs to maximise their effectiveness

- are we taking full account of cultural contexts in designing programs for Indigenous people (cf. Larkin 2006)

- are we building evaluation into the foundations of all programs, and are we taking the opportunities to learn from these findings even when the results are discomforting?

For the research sector, some of the key questions might include

- are we working on the most important problems (have we taken account of the views of policymakers, practitioners and program clients)

- have we systematically involved other sectors (who will be users of and audiences for research) in our consideration of the knowledge base for assessing program effectiveness

- are we working at an appropriate scale (micro or macro; local or regional; single or multiple issues) that will be of interest to policy and practice partners

- have we summarised our research findings in ways that draw out the implications for practitioners and decision makers

- will our findings be accessible and intelligible to other sectors and to the media?

For the practitioner sector, some of the key questions might include

- are we taking steps to document the impacts of our work with particular groups of clients as a basis for collective discussion of evidence-based practice (cf. Mullen et al. 2008; Simons 2004)

- are we creating or using frameworks for linking client casework to broader program and policy considerations (cf. Proctor and Rosen 2008)

- are we gathering evidence concerning the interlinked nature of social problems and successful measures for addressing such complex issues

- are we utilising and strengthening community networks on key issues (cf. Foster-Fishman et al. 2001)

- are we utilising new forums for continuing review of 'best-practice' approaches and attention to 'prospective' new approaches

- are we inviting policy and research colleagues into these forums?

Tackling big issues through collaboration

It has been demonstrated in many contexts that professional knowledge bases are the important building blocks of improved understanding, but that the 'silos' of professional knowledge are also obstacles to the diffusion of innovation (Dopson and Fitzgerald 2005; Ferlie et al. 2005). I have argued that if the challenge for collective engagement is to focus on *high-priority complex issues* then the task goes well beyond casual networking and information exchange. This is a strategic challenge requiring large-scale resources and collective energy, a focus on agenda setting and moving from knowledge to action. Pooling the insights of diverse experts from each sector (research, policy, practice) is only the beginning of a collaborative process that requires a significant degree of coordination (see Figure 8.1). For example, the Australian Research Alliance for Children and Youth (ARACY 2004) 'collaboration framework' envisages a carefully designed process among key players. This collaborative process would require the participants to define key issues, take stock of expert knowledge, evaluate the impediments to progress, recommend fresh approaches and unpack the implications for policy, practice and research.

Figure 8.1 The interactive hub of collaboration

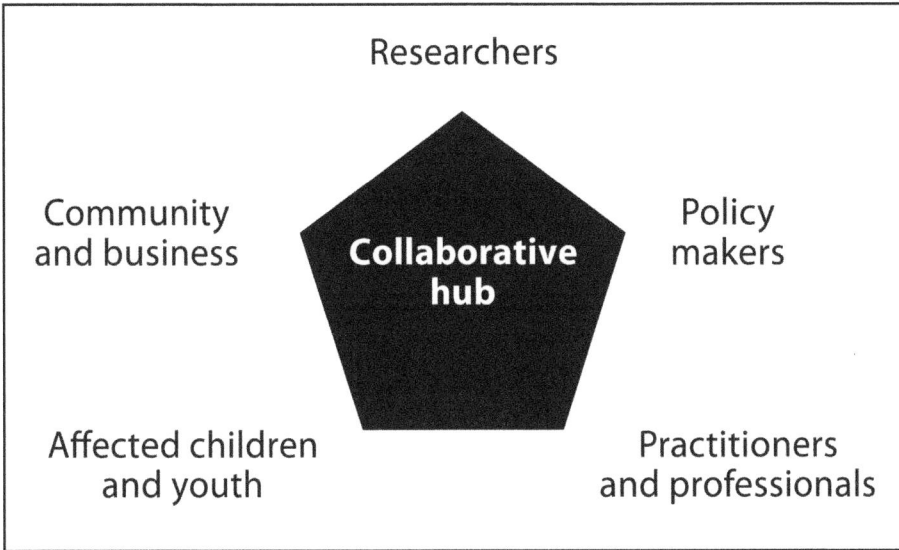

Patterns of *knowledge sharing* across the sectors (research–policy–practice) need to be appropriate to the specific contexts of joint work. It is necessary to construct these relationships in ways appropriate for each problem context and to recognise that partnering arrangements can be constructed in diverse ways. In principle, the focus of joint work could be highly varied, such as

- devising and testing different 'scenarios' for the use of knowledge and strategy in pursuit of policy objectives (cf. Oreszczyn and Carr 2008)

- field testing a pilot program, delivered by a mix of non-governmental organisations (NGOs) and public agencies, funded by government and evaluated by researchers

- documenting the outcomes of a mature program devised and delivered by NGOs, funded by corporate philanthropy and initially evaluated by consultants

- fundamental reassessment of why government programs for Indigenous communities have so often failed (requiring a sustained 'think tank' forum informed by many forms of knowledge)

- documenting and disseminating promising examples of local initiatives, perhaps led by practitioners, that appear to have produced positive outcomes

- assessing the strengths and limitations of inter-agency coordination and intergovernmental cooperation as strategic frameworks for the improvement of government services.

The knowledge-sharing challenges in each of these examples are rather different. Knowledge-sharing strategies and processes can be judged as more or less 'effective' only in relation to stated purposes. What works well for one purpose, or in one context, might be insufficient elsewhere. One example of effective knowledge sharing is the Inala Program in south-east Queensland, where an innovative prevention and support program was designed and implemented through a partnership between government agencies, a community-based NGO (Mission Australia) and a university research team (Freiberg et al. 2005; Homel et al. 2006). The focus on developmental prevention and early intervention for a group of preschool children from disadvantaged families required close collaboration between the children and their parents/carers, the teachers, professionals providing support services, government agency staff and the research team. This multi-layered approach has produced some positive outcomes, which in turn influenced the design of other national and regional programs focusing on the early years and readiness for school.

The common intent in all such initiatives is to establish shared ownership of new thinking and new strategies. Knowledge brokering can play a vital role. It involves active strategies among relevant actors for sharing and negotiating understandings about problems, evidence bases and solutions. Building strong relationships and participatory processes is essential for knowledge brokering.

Much has been written about the growing role of influential individuals who provide a service in *bridging and linking* between groups or institutions. These individuals have a capacity to build bridges, span boundaries and otherwise facilitate the translation and adoption of ideas (for example, Tsui 2006; Williams 2002). In an increasingly networked and mediated environment, linking and bridging roles are common and necessary. Innovative organisations will increasingly seek to embed such roles in their senior teams to promote productive interchange and partnering. While there are real benefits from interactive and collaborative approaches, there are, however, also costs.

Investing in knowledge sharing across disciplines and sectors has real costs, especially in higher *transaction costs* of collaborative approaches. These are centred primarily on the time and effort required for engagement, communication and goal-setting discussions across disciplines and sectors, which are a necessary prerequisite to project planning and implementation (Metcalfe et al. 2006). Similarly, an organisation contemplating various cooperative options for pursuing its goals will need to assess whether the potential benefits are outweighed by the administrative and communication costs of 'cooperation' with others (White 2005).

Partly in response to this issue, a new breed of network organisations has emerged (such as ARACY), dedicated to knowledge brokering and knowledge sharing on behalf of their members. This network format provides an economy of collective effort to reap some of the rewards of collective action. The ideal situation might be that every organisation in each sector would redesign its internal arrangements in order to improve its communications, participate in regular dialogue with others and share in new processes of joint thinking and action. It is, however, unrealistic to expect all organisations to develop new capacities for innovative and shared thinking. Involvement in network organisations is therefore a useful and convenient way to take some first steps towards these new capacities. Assisting in the establishment of new forums for the latter activities is an indicator of how far such organisations might have changed.

Many groups are also undertaking more specific forms of partnering activities. Longer-term partnerships are needed to build trust around high-quality research on matters of mutually agreed importance. A successful partnership of this type will focus on the 'co-production' of useful knowledge. Interchange of personnel might be useful to promote the exchange of ideas and understandings; and cross-appointments to the advisory bodies of other organisations can also assist. Research partnerships—for example, Australian Research Council (ARC) Linkage grants—can be useful. Contract research involving several parties also has inherent risks—for example, delays and complexities arising from the need for multi-party contractual agreements; the lack of continuity of key staff (rapid turnover in policy and program positions can undermine a coherent sense of direction); and the long time frames before the delivery of usable results.

Dilemmas for research relevance

There is increasing pressure for academic researchers to ensure their applied work is more responsive and attuned to the perspectives of other sectors (Davies et al. 2000; Nutley et al. 2007). Social research is of a higher standard when it takes account of the views of practitioners and policymakers. For example, if social research projects ignore the views of practitioners and service providers, such analyses are likely to be deficient, since they are unlikely to be alert to the success factors underlying effective interventions. And yet, the incentive structures and rewards for academic research give priority to prestigious publications and success in competitive grants. These criteria of success tend to work against giving higher priority to social relevance. (A partial exception is in the medical or technical sciences to the extent that new insights can be linked to commercial applications.)

In the human services and the social care sectors, there has been a huge research literature establishing the key risk factors and protective factors for the healthy development of young people. The shift from knowledge to action is, however, constrained at many points. Programs based on technical advances (for example, immunisation) are readily implemented. More complex programs, however, addressing multiple related problems have been difficult to design and implement with long-term funding. The importance of proceeding cautiously through local pilot projects and local evaluations is well established. Nevertheless, it has been difficult to develop large-scale programs that are well informed by continuing social research and feedback from practical experience. This is perhaps the greatest challenge for research relevance and perhaps the greatest potential contribution of a collaborative model for cross-sector strategy development.

If policymakers believe that academic research is abstract or irrelevant, academic researchers will be further sidelined and the research consultancy industry will win most of the applied social research contracts. If, however, social research 'over-compensates' by becoming highly instrumental—tailoring research to fit the current requirements of a funding agency—this also has major dangers. Academic research is increasingly required to demonstrate two forms of value that pull in different directions: excellence in quality/rigour and relevance to the priority concerns of funders and stakeholders. The ideal outcome would be high-quality research on topics of high importance. Importantly, however, judgments concerning the *impact* or relevance of research will continue to depend on the views of other sectors—government, business, community, and so on. If a major goal of researchers is to increase the *utilisation* of research findings (Amara et al. 2004; Huberman 1994; Weiss 1979), this would require researchers to take an active approach that goes beyond mere dissemination or diffusion of research papers (Lavis et al. 2003). Active marketing, engagement and influencing would be necessary, but not just around a research report. The most powerful methods for long-term influence are likely to be knowledge-sharing approaches built around major continuing themes or problems.

Conclusions

Shared thinking comes from a partnering approach. We have noted that personal relationships and face-to-face interactions are very important and should be encouraged. Even more significant, however, is the need to boost the sense of 'ownership' of applied research directions and findings. Research itself requires a more integrated approach (Bammer 2006). Moving towards a co-production model, new thinking for joint research could extend to designing research questions about policy and practice jointly among the stakeholders, funders and representatives of service users.

The development of more strategic approaches to service improvement requires new network arrangements to promote better communication and shared perspectives across the professions and across the policy–research–practice sectors (Scott and Thurston 2003; Wandersman et al. 2008; Weinstein et al. 2003). For these new forums to have greater impact, it is important to encourage the growth of 'learning cultures' within organisations as well as across organisations. Hence it is necessary to influence the organisational climate within agencies at a senior level, so that they are more *receptive* to dialogue about new approaches and more receptive to the findings of jointly agreed research programs. Similar changes are necessary in the research cultures of academic and non-governmental organisations.

The process requirements for successful collaboration seem to include inclusive participation, mutual respect for each other's knowledge and values, support for members to participate fully in the broader network, clarity on the rules for joint decision making and effective leadership roles. The sustainability of networks— their capacity to thrive and adapt over a long period—is important (Head 2006). Collaborative networks seem to be the best method currently available to address the inherent complexity and fragmentation embedded in social problems and the best way to achieve outcomes in a contested policy environment (Head 2008b). The criteria for judging the effectiveness of collaborative networks are, however, likely to be divergent, owing to the different views and interests of participants (Provan and Milward 2001). In a networked world, knowledge transmission is no longer sufficient to generate a new consensus around goals and strategies. We need to develop our knowledge-brokering and knowledge-sharing capabilities to tackle the big strategic issues we face.

References

Amara, N., Ouimet, M. and Landry, R. 2004, 'New evidence on instrumental, conceptual, and symbolic utilization of university research in government agencies', *Science Communication*, vol. 26, no. 1, pp. 75–106.

Australian Research Alliance for Children and Youth (ARACY) 2004, *ARACY Framework for Collaboration*, Australian Research Alliance for Children and Youth, Canberra, viewed 3 May 2010, <http://www.aracy.org.au/publicationDocuments/TOP_ARACY_Framework_for_Collaboration_2005.pdf>

Australian Research Alliance for Children and Youth (ARACY) 2008, *Report Card on the Wellbeing of Young Australians*, Australian Research Alliance for Children and Youth, Canberra.

Bammer, G. 2006, 'A systematic approach to integration in research', *Integration Insights*, no. 1, ANU College of Medicine and Health Sciences, Canberra, viewed 3 May 2010, <http://i2s.anu.edu.au/sites/default/files/integration-insights/integration-insight_1.pdf>

Bowen, S. and Zwi, A. B. 2005, 'Pathways to "evidence-informed" policy and practice: a framework for action', *PLoS Medicine*, vol. 2, no. 7 (e166), pp. 100–5.

Brownson, R. C., Royer, C., Ewing, R. and McBride, T. D. 2006, 'Researchers and policymakers: travelers in parallel universes', *American Journal of Preventive Medicine*, vol. 30, no. 2, pp. 164–72.

Davies, H., Nutley, S. and Smith, P. (eds) 2000, *What Works? Evidence-based policy and practice in public services*, Policy Press, Bristol.

Dopson, S. and Fitzgerald, L. (eds) 2005, *Knowledge to Action? Evidence-based health care in context*, Oxford University Press, UK.

Feldman, P. H. and Kane, R. L. 2003, 'Strengthening research to improve the practice and management of long-term care', *Milbank Quarterly*, vol. 81, no. 2, pp. 179–220.

Ferlie, E., Fitzgerald, L., Wood, M. and Hawkins, C. 2005, 'The nonspread of innovations: the mediating role of professionals', *Academy of Management Journal*, vol. 48, no. 1, pp. 117–34.

Foster-Fishman, P., Berkowitz, S., Lounsbury, D., Jacobson, S. and Allen, N. 2001, 'Building collaborative capacity in community coalitions: a review and integrative framework', *American Journal of Community Psychology*, vol. 29, no. 2, pp. 241–61.

Freiberg, K., Homel, R., Batchelor, S., Carr, A., Hay, I. Elias, G., Teague, R. and Lamb, C. 2005, 'Pathways to participation: a community-based developmental prevention project in Australia', *Children and Society*, vol. 19, no. 2, pp. 144–57.

Head, B. W. 2006, *Effective Collaboration*, July, Australian Research Alliance for Children and Youth, Canberra, viewed 3 May 2010, <http://www.aracy.org.au/publicationDocuments/TOP_Effective_Collaboration_2006.pdf>

Head, B. W. 2008a, 'Three lenses of evidence based policy', *Australian Journal of Public Administration*, vol. 67, no. 1, pp. 1–11.

Head, B. W. 2008b, 'Assessing network-based collaborations: effectiveness for whom?', *Public Management Review*, vol. 10, no. 6, pp. 733–49.

Head, B. W. and Stanley, F. J. 2007, 'Evidence-based advocacy', *International Journal of Adolescent Medicine and Health*, vol. 19, no. 3, pp. 255–62.

Homel, R., Freiberg, K., Lamb, C., Leech, M., Carr, A., Hampshire, A., Hay, I., Elias, G., Manning, M., Teague, R. and Batchelor, S. 2006, *The Pathways to Prevention Project: The first five years, 1999–2004*, Mission Australia and Key Centre for Ethics, Law, Justice and Governance, Griffith University, Brisbane.

Huberman, M. 1994, 'Research utilization: the state of the art', *Knowledge and Policy: The international journal of knowledge transfer and utilization*, vol. 7, no. 4, pp. 13–33.

Larkin, S. 2006, 'Evidence-based policy making in Aboriginal and Torres Strait Islander health', *Australian Aboriginal Studies*, vol. 2, pp. 17–26.

Lavis, J. N., Robertson, D., Woodside, J. M., McLeod, C. B. and Abelson, J. 2003, 'How can research organizations more effectively transfer research knowledge to decision makers?', *Milbank Quarterly*, vol. 81, no. 2, pp. 221–48.

Lewig, K., Arney, F. and Scott, D. 2006, 'Closing the research–policy and research–practice gaps: ideas for child and family services', *Family Matters*, vol. 74, pp. 12–19.

Lomas, J. 1990, 'Finding audiences, changing beliefs: the structure of research use in Canadian health policy', *Journal of Health Politics, Policy and Law*, vol. 15, no. 3, pp. 525–42.

Lomas, J. 2000, 'Using "linkage and exchange" to move research into policy at a Canadian foundation', *Health Affairs*, vol. 19, no. 3, pp. 236–40.

McAdam, R., Mason, B. and McCrory, J. 2007, 'Exploring the dichotomies within the tacit knowledge literature: towards a process of tacit knowing in organizations', *Journal of Knowledge Management*, vol. 11, no. 2, pp. 43–59.

Metcalfe, J., Riedlinger, M., Pisarski, A. and Gardner, J. 2006, *Collaborating Across the Sectors*, Council for the Humanities, Arts and Social Sciences, Canberra.

Mullen, E. J., Bledsoe, S. E. and Bellamy, J. L. 2008, 'Implementing evidence-based social work practice', *Research on Social Work Practice*, vol. 18, no. 4, pp. 325–38.

Nutley, S., Walter, I. and Davies, H. 2007, *Using Evidence: How research can inform public services*, Policy Press, Bristol.

Oreszczyn, S. and Carr, S. 2008, 'Improving the link between policy research and practice', *Qualitative Research*, vol. 8, no. 4, pp. 473–97.

Proctor, E. and Rosen, A. 2008, 'From knowledge production to implementation', *Research on Social Work Practice*, vol. 18, no. 4, pp. 285–91.

Provan, K. G. and Milward, H. B. 2001, 'Do networks really work? A framework for evaluating public sector organisational networks', *Public AdministrationReview*, vol. 61, no. 4, pp. 414–23.

Salveron, M., Arney, F. and Scott, D. 2006, 'Sowing the seeds of innovation: ideas for child and family services', *Family Matters*, vol. 73, pp. 39–45.

Schon, D. A. 1983, *The Reflective Practitioner: How professionals think in action*, Basic Books, New York.

Schon, D. A. and Rein, M. 1994, *Frame Reflection: Toward the resolution of intractable policy controversies*, Basic Books, New York.

Schorr, L. B. 2003, *Determining 'What Works' in Social Programs and Social Policies: Toward a more inclusive knowledge base*, Brookings Institution, Washington, DC.

Scott, C. M. and Thurston, W. E. (eds) 2003, *Collaboration in Context*, University of Calgary, Alberta.

Shonkoff, J. P. 2000, 'Science, policy, and practice: three cultures in search of a shared mission', *Child Development*, vol. 71, no. 1, pp. 181–7.

Simons, H. 2004, 'Utilizing evaluation evidence to enhance professional practice', *Evaluation*, vol. 10, no. 4, pp. 410–29.

Tsui, L. 2006, *A Handbook for Knowledge Sharing*, Community–University Partnership for Study of Children Youth and Families, Alberta.

Wandersman, A., Duffy, J., Flaspohler, P., Noonan, R., Lubell, K., Stillman, L., Blachman, M., Dunville, R. and Saul, J. 2008, 'Bridging the gap between prevention research and practice', *American Journal of Community Psychology*, vol. 41, nos 3–4, pp. 171–81.

Weinstein, J., Whittington, C. and Leiba, T. (eds) 2003, *Collaboration in Social Work Practice*, Jessica Kingsley, London.

Weiss, C. H. 1979, 'The many meanings of research utilization', *Public Administration Review*, vol. 39, no. 5, pp. 426–31.

Wenger, E. 1998, *Communities of Practice*, Cambridge University Press, UK.

White, S. 2005, 'Cooperation costs, governance choice and alliance evolution', *Journal of Management Studies*, vol. 42, no. 7, pp. 1383–412.

Williams, P. 2002, 'The competent boundary spanner', *Public Administration*, vol. 80, no. 1, pp. 103–24.

9. Knowledge, power and politics

Michael Moore

In 1597, British philosopher Francis Bacon, in meditating on religion and heresies, recognised the integral relationship between knowledge and power with his statement 'knowledge is power'. Although community benefit can often be derived from sharing knowledge, Bacon's insight helps explain why politicians and their bureaucrats are often reluctant to make knowledge broadly available. The pervasive approach to sharing of knowledge within the bureaucratic and political arenas is one of reluctance. It is a measured and considered process that is carefully designed to avoid undermining the use of power.

There is invariably a tension between different groups and individuals who would exercise power in the political sphere. In a liberal democracy, such tensions are exercised most obviously in the cabinet, on the floor of the parliament and in the committees. Power, however, is not restricted to those in government but can be shared by other elected members, powerful lobby groups, the media and the bureaucracy. Knowledge and understanding of issues, systems and people provide keys to successful lobbying and use of power. Furthermore, the environment in which policy decisions are taken is rarely straightforward.

Edwards (2001:3) writes: 'Policy environments are full of complexities, usually involving a diverse range of players coming from different perspectives and spawning a host of unexpected events. It is therefore very unlikely that circumstance would permit anything approaching a classical rationality in the decision making process.'

Edwards' contention is that a systematic approach to policy development can deliver better outcomes. Within the context of such policy process complexities, however, key players are keen to protect information. Information might persuade others to a view that does not sit easily with the perspective that they bring to the policy process and must therefore be protected for use in a manner that suits their own purposes.

Although hoarding of information to reinforce political positions is common, sharing of knowledge is not foreign to the political process and has been well established in the parliamentary committee inquiry process. One of the great strengths of parliamentary committees has been their ability to find information and knowledge and to share it through appropriate reporting of their findings to the people via the parliaments. Harris (2001:605) writes: 'Committee inquiries enable Members to be better informed about community views but in simply undertaking an inquiry committees may promote public debate.' In Australia, senate committees in particular, and their counterparts in other parliaments, have become a key mechanism for sharing knowledge. As such, they are also instruments for sharing power.

In contrast with the approach of backbenchers within the committee system, under a Westminster government, having been drawn from elected members of the parliament, a cabinet invariably sets about consolidating its own power. One of the techniques used by governments to secure knowledge and therefore to consolidate their power is 'cabinet-in-confidence'. The use of this instrument demonstrates the importance of the relationship between the power of the executive arm of government and knowledge that is kept from others in the parliament and from the general public. Documents marked 'cabinet-in-confidence' are not available publicly for long periods unless released at the time by the head of the cabinet (in Australia, the prime minister in the federal government, the premier in state governments and chief minister in territory governments). It is common in Australia for 'cabinet-in-confidence' documents to be held for up to 30 years before being released. In Queensland, the documents are held for 30 years while in the newest jurisdiction, the Australian Capital Territory, 10 years is considered adequate.

'Cabinet-in-confidence' documents that are released after more than one-quarter of a century provide some interesting insights into decisions of the time. The majority is, however, made up of mundane administrative matters and have largely been suppressed to protect the public servants and cabinet members of the time from any risk of controversy. In issues of security and policy development, there could be some reason for governments to hold on to documents for such periods. The reality is, however, that the use of this technique is primarily about avoiding the sharing of knowledge and, with it, avoiding the risk of having to share power.

When doubt exists about what information may or may not be available, it is difficult to question the decision a minister makes. It is safer for a minister—and the bureaucrats—if it is not known what information was available at the time. Should all the information be made available, it would be possible to carry out a full analysis of the decision-making process and with it the competency of the minister and those who advised in the process.

The case of Mohamed Haneef, who was arrested in Australia, held and interrogated for three weeks before being allowed to go free, provides a specific example to demonstrate the tension involved in the use of knowledge as power within the political context (BBC 2007). The struggle between the government, which was trying to keep knowledge to itself, and the lawyers headed by Peter Russo, who were using the courts to make knowledge available, provides an illustration of the importance of knowledge as power in the political context. The Australian Government was notified by British intelligence services that Haneef was a person of interest in an investigation of acts of terrorism in the United Kingdom. Information was able to be cosseted for political purposes using legislation and arguments about the need to protect the country from terrorists. The risk of inappropriate use of intelligence provided by international colleagues provided a further argument for confining knowledge to be used as wished by the government for its own purposes.

The Liberal government, only months away from a general election, saw the opportunity to use fear and uncertainty as tools to win votes. The police were under pressure to be successful in dealing with terrorism. The dominant discourse of the time was that the government had to be seen to take whatever action was necessary to protect the people. The democratic checks and balances, however, proved a challenge to the government about how they could use their own knowledge. When the courts indicated that the information presented by the police was not enough to keep Haneef detained, bail was granted. Immediately, the Immigration Minister, The Hon Kevin Andrews, stepped in to continue the detention through the application of a different set of laws: the immigration legislation.

Andrews argued that the police had provided him with information (which he could not share) that left him with no choice but to keep Haneef in detention. The political and media pressure was so great that Andrews eventually released a part of the transcript of a chat-room conversation between Haneef and his brother. It rapidly became clear to the public and the media that the information had been taken out of context. The evidence was as unconvincing for the public as it had been for the magistrate who granted bail. It was not difficult, however, to understand why the minister—who was looking for a specific outcome in the election context—would have been persuaded by the words to detain Haneef. Andrews found himself sandwiched between the media and the public on the one hand, who were still critical of the information, and the police on the other, who were critical of the release of the information. Andrews announced that he had further information that he could not release. Supposedly, this further information was of great significance in dealing with international terrorism and if he were to release it, it might not be able to be used in court should further charges be laid. The suppression of this information provided Andrews with the power needed to maintain his position.

The police understood the importance of holding information to themselves as it provided uncertainty and retained power in the hands of the government. Andrews was somewhat more vulnerable, as defence lawyers had been selectively leaking the only information that was reaching a hungry media. The further difficulty for Andrews was that, unlike the police, he and the Prime Minister would probably have to answer questions on the matter in the subsequent sittings of parliament. There would also be the opportunity for some exposure if documents were requested under the *Freedom of Information Act* (although much of this information would be able to be suppressed as it had to do with terrorism). The other accountability to be faced by a government would be the establishment of a parliamentary committee of inquiry. In previous decades, this technique had been used frequently by the senate committees—which were not tied to the government agenda—to expose governments that attempted to hide information. With a government majority in the Senate, however, this accountability mechanism was likely to fail. It would not be until 1 July 2008, with the swearing in of the newly elected senators so that no party had a majority in the Senate, that an opportunity would be available for a senate inquiry.

Although Andrews and Prime Minister, John Howard, had seen an electoral opportunity, the Haneef case in fact added to a loss of trust in the government. One drawback of failure to share knowledge is that it plays an important part in diminishing social capital. Although the term might not be immediately apparent, social capital should be well understood by governments. It comprises a series of important facets including knowledge, language, trust and understanding. According to Christensen and Levinson (2003:2), 'Finally, social capital can be measured by the fraction of people who trust one another. Generalized trust acts as a form of social glue, fostering participation in politics, and facilitating bridging across ethnic, racial and class lines.'

The level of trust in political institutions is steadily diminishing. *The Age* newspaper (2004) reported that a 'study of voter attitudes on social and political issues conducted by Irving Saulwick for *The Sunday Age* found 33 per cent of voters say that they seldom or never trust political leaders in Canberra (while 41 per cent say they sometimes trust them)'.

It is not clear whether or not the sharing of information and knowledge would assist in building trust and, with it, social capital. As illustrated by the Haneef case, however, the suppression of knowledge appears to undermine social capital. When a parliamentary committee report carries a dissenting view, the substantive report usually receives much more attention. It becomes clear to the media that there is tension between members and the difference of opinion makes good copy. A minority view attached to a report is usually added to air a dissenting view. Sometimes, particularly when the government does not hold the numbers in the committee, the dissenting view is a political tool to ensure that the member is not too critical of his/her own government. Conversely, when the government has the numbers, a dissenting report could be the only way that opposition members can voice an opinion. The most powerful and influential reports are those that carry no dissenting voice. The committees have the power to perform functions such as 'finding out the facts of a case or issue, examining witnesses, sifting evidence and drawing up reasoned conclusions' (Harris 2001:605). Even these committees, however, do have the power to withhold information, expunge material from evidence and suppress parts or all of a report (Harris 2001:664). Even in the system designed to open governments and expose knowledge and ideas, the importance of knowledge as political power is well understood.

Governments have recognised the importance of trust as part of delivering an effective government. In the Australian Capital Territory Legislative Assembly, the concept of *social capital* was used as a cornerstone of the budget that was released in 2000. The Treasurer at the time identified the concept as 'the fourth dimension of an economy. It adds to the market concept of financial capital which covers property and equipment; environmental capital such as land, farming and mining; and, human capital that includes the skills and education of the workforce' (Humphries 2000:7).

A booklet was developed as part of the budget papers to explain the concept and why the government took it so seriously as that time.[1] Building trust is extraordinarily difficult when knowledge—and with it power—is not being shared to any extent. Hiding information and restricting access invariably raise suspicion and reduce the level of trust. The cabinet handbook of the government of the Australian Capital Territory sets out a series of security measures to protect cabinet information ranging from national security through to the protection of ministers. This government releases documents after a period of 10 years—provided that the current cabinet does not object to any information being released (Cabinet Office 2007:22–3). Even though the government tried to build trust in this way, when it was given the opportunity to reduce the time for the suppression of cabinet-in-confidence documents through the Executive Documents Release Bill 2000, neither the government (Liberal) nor the alternative government (Labor) could take the necessary step as indicated by the votes of all Members of the Assembly (*Hansard*, 21 June 2001:2348).

The frustration that many feel about government processes and the failure to share knowledge grow out of a lack of understanding of how power is used to guarantee the restriction of knowledge. Wayne Parsons provides a clear insight into this issue in attempting to analyse these types of concerns:

> The real power in the policy process is the power to make non-decisions; that is, the capacity of one group to prevent ideas, concerns, interests and problems of another group getting 'on' the agenda in the first place.

---

1 Please note that the author was a minister in this government at the time and was the force behind adoption of the concept of social capital as part of the budget strategy.

> Furthermore, this position may be extended to say that, if we want to understand how problems are defined, and agendas set, we have to go much deeper than the surface relations of power, into the way in which values and beliefs of people are shaped. (Parsons 1995:86)

Mal Brough, the then Minister for Families, Community Services and Indigenous Affairs, with the support of Prime Minister Howard, launched an extraordinary intervention into the control of Indigenous communities in the Northern Territory on 21 June 2007 (Howard 2007). Howard argued that his responsible minister had brought the issue squarely on to the agenda: 'It is our view that if it hadn't been for the persistence of Mr Brough in elevating this as an issue, the inquiry conducted by Rex Wild and Pat Anderson would never have been commissioned' (Howard 2007).

The concern he raised was primarily about the widespread sexual and physical abuse of children. Within weeks, there were hundreds of health checks being carried out by the task force that arrived in remote communities within the territory. In August, Brough tabled legislation in the Parliament to allow a further range of activities and interventions by the federal government while carrying out its plan in the Northern Territory.

The struggle over knowledge in this case was really for the dominant discourse. There had been previous attempts to make knowledge available but politicians and the media had not heard them. The most prominent of these was the Royal Commission into Aboriginal Deaths in Custody, which reported in 1991 (Johnston 1991). Indigenous leader Noel Pearson had grown in influence with the Howard government and particularly with Brough. Pearson had a particular 'take' on the causes and solutions, which was hotly contested by others. Pearson's 'knowledge' became the dominant discourse. Within a very short time, it became the accepted form of knowledge for the government and most of the media at the expense of much other information about underlying causes and the ingredients of successful solutions.

Labor's spokeswoman, Jenny Macklin, in addressing the legislation, identified the reason for Opposition support with the comment: 'We believe that these laws are designed to protect especially vulnerable Aboriginal children' (Macklin 2007:91).

She also identified the limitations of the Opposition support for the bill by applying a simple test to all parts of the legislation: 'Will it improve the safety and security of our children in a practical way?' (Macklin 2007:92).

The question that is pertinent to sharing knowledge is why had people not acted until now, especially if it were true to identify the 'litany of reports'? Parsons' insights assist the understanding of what now seems to have been culpable neglect by state and territory governments and by federal ministers before Brough. Perhaps they did not have the wherewithal to look beyond what was politically correct. With the wisdom of hindsight, it would appear that powerful lobby groups had kept the understanding from general knowledge that this abuse was so pervasive. It provided a springboard, however, for launching the Pearson discourse. It is true that there were many arguments against such an intervention, including: fear of 'whitefella' intervention, communities must take responsibility for their own, partnerships are the key way to develop understanding and this will just colour attitudes to Indigenous people.

Independent of an individual's view of whether the intervention is good or bad, what is really clear is that one powerful lobby group has been able to ensure that another view is not generally considered either in the community or within the political sphere. The announcement was made within the context of an impending election. As such, many have dismissed the intervention as a political tool. Perhaps it was. Perhaps, however, there was a genuine concern that had come to the attention of Brough and the impending election provided the tool to put the issue fairly on the agenda in such a way that arguments to the contrary would be difficult. In the final outcome, the decision that was made was political and a powerful though selective discourse was used to support it. This is not new. Ron Sackville (1979:6) explained the gaping crevice between knowledge and evidence on one hand and decision making on the other in his Royal Commission report: 'The most persuasive misunderstanding that affects a Commission such as ours is the belief that crucial policy questions can be resolved by carefully weighing up the scientific, medical and statistical evidence.'

Although knowledge and evidence can be important in government processes, they form a part of the decision-making process. They are not always a crucial part.

Mal Brough was attempting to establish a specific understanding or 'knowledge' of this issue. Noel Pearson, who is a member of the Bama Bagaarrmugu people from the Kalpowa and Jeanie River area of south-eastern Cape York, had been attempting to share his concerns and approach for some time. The Cape York Partnership web site sets out his background and concern about an issue that he has been pursuing for a number of years:

> As well as [being] the Director of Cape York Partnerships and voluntary team leader of *Every Child Is Special*, Noel is the Director of the Cape York Institute for Policy and Leadership [<www.cyi.org.au>] which aims to drive policy innovation and move to include a model of active

Indigenous participation in public policy debates. Noel continues to work as an advisor to Indigenous organisations in Cape York. (Cape York Partnerships 2007)

As far back as 2003, Pearson had been trying to get attention from the government to share his view of knowledge about social conditions impacting on the lives of the Indigenous people of his area. He prepared a paper for a round-table discussion with Prime Minister Howard that included the following principle: 'Avoid reliance on experts from the "Aboriginal industry"' (Pearson 2003).

In knowledge-sharing terms, this point identifies Pearson's concern about being able to share his view broadly. Indeed, it would be another four years, a minister prepared to take a huge risk and the context of an election before his suggestions would come into mainstream discussion and eventually become the dominant discourse. In 2003, Pearson identified the 'Aboriginal industry' in a way that suggested frustration about not being able to present his solutions without having the views contained by such a powerful lobby group. Even the words he uses in his description of those with an alternative view as the 'Aboriginal industry' illustrates the importance of holding on to the dominant discourse in influencing governments.

Although people such as Pearson had been trying to communicate the idea of a national crisis for years, the intervention launched by the Prime Minister seemed to come as a surprise to many—particularly those in the 'Aboriginal industry'. The frustration of such 'industry' leaders came out as they met the then Opposition Leader, Kevin Rudd. Attempts to challenge the discourse were largely unsuccessful. Former chief executive of the Aboriginal and Torres Strait Islander Commission (ATSIC), Pat Turner, vigorously attacked the process: 'It is very, very disheartening that the Government has been able to treat everybody… with no respect…I've never seen such an abuse of power in parliament' (Karvelas 2007). She was accompanied by former Northern Territory Indigenous Affairs Minister John Ah Kit, who stated: 'This is about the beginning of the end of Aboriginal culture, it is in some ways genocide' (Karvelas 2007).

It is clear that the alternative discourse to that being put by Pearson for many years was now being lost under the pressure of a single view emphasising the importance of protection of vulnerable children. No doubt, Ah Kit would feel both the frustration of not leading the debate and the vulnerability of not taking on this sort of protection when he had responsibility at the time he was minister. Perhaps this accounts for a slight softening of the approach taken by Turner and Ah Kit when he stated, 'We all agree that there needs to be changes in the Territory but we need to be involved in the consultation process' (Karvelas 2007). The consultation process is about being involved in the sharing of knowledge and the sharing of power and the hope of being able to bring other factors into the discourse. In the end, the political decision maker is responsible for taking action but the knowledge and understanding of the issues come through a process of negotiation and recognition of those who have control of the knowledge and those who are being excluded from the process.

This series of examples illustrates the close link between knowledge and power. For those who are seeking to improve the health of communities, groups and individuals, it is critical that knowledge and understanding are shared. When this happens, decisions that are taken are recognised as being mutually derived and mutually beneficial. Such decisions need to be made, however, with an understanding of how power and knowledge are used. At times, they are shared for the general community good. At other times—even with a perception that it is for community benefit—knowledge (and with it power) is restricted to those on a 'need-to-know' basis and those who control the dominant view. The challenge, therefore, is to minimise the restriction of knowledge and to maximise the sharing of information.

References

The Age 2004, 'How to succeed in politics', Editorial, *The Age*, 5 September 2004, viewed 10 August 2007, <http://www.theage.com.au/articles/2004/09/04/1094234072746.html?from=storylhs>

Bacon, F. 1597, *Religious Meditations, of Heresies*, viewed 3 August 2007, <http://www.quotationspage.com/quote/2060.html>

British Broadcasting Corporation (BBC) 2007, 'Haneef terrorism charges dropped', *BBC*, 27 July 2007, viewed 12 August 2007, <http://news.bbc.co.uk/1/hi/world/asia-pacific/6918569.stm>

Cabinet Office 2007, *Directions on Cabinet Procedure*, Cabinet Handbook, Government of the Australian Capital Territory, Canberra, viewed 10 August 2007, <http://www.cmd.act.gov.au/__data/assets/pdf_file/0005/113585/cabinet-handbook.pdf>

Cape York Partnerships 2007, *Cape York Partnerships*, viewed 16 May 2010, <http://www.capeyorkpartnerships.com/noel-pearson>

Christensen, K. and Levinson, D. (eds) 2003, 'Trends in social capital', *Encyclopaedia of Community: From the village to the virtual world*, Sage, Thousand Oaks, Calif., viewed 10 August 2007, <http://econrsss.anu.edu.au/~aleigh/pdf/TrendsInSK.pdf>

Edwards, M. 2001, *Social Policy, Public Policy: From problem to practice*, Allen & Unwin, Crows Nest, NSW.

Hansard of the Australian Capital Territory, viewed 16 May 2010, <www. hansard.act.gov.au/hansard/2001/pdfs/20010621.pdf>

Harris, I. (ed.) 2001, *House of Representatives Practice*, Fourth edn, Department of the House of Representatives, Canberra.

Howard, J. 2007, Indigenous emergency, Interview transcript, Joint Press Conference with the Hon. Mal Brough, Minister for Families, Community Services and Indigenous Affairs, Canberra, 21 June 2007, viewed 16 May 2010, <http://parlinfo.aph.gov.au/parlInfo/download/media/pressrel/8XFN6/ upload_binary/8xfn61.pdf;fileType=application/pdf#search=%22ZD4|R eporterIdZD4|SpeakerIdZD4%20brough,%20mal,%20mp%20media%20 no%20howard,%20john,%20mp%22>

Humphries, G. 2000, *Building social capital*, ACT Budget Paper 5, 2000–01, ACT Legislative Assembly, Canberra, viewed 3 August 2007, <http://www. treasury.act.gov.au/budget/budget2000/bp5/bp5.pdf>

Johnston, E. 1991, *Royal Commission into Aboriginal Deaths in Custody*, viewed 16 May 2010, <http://www.austlii.com/au/other/IndigLRes/rciadic/>

Karvelas, P. 2007, 'Labor backs "genocide" policy', *The Australian*, 8 August 2007, viewed 16 May 2007, <http://www.theaustralian.news.com.au/ story/0,25197,22207932-5013404,00.html>

Macklin, J. 2007, Hansard second reading speech, Federal Parliament, Canberra, 7 August 2007, viewed 20 May 2010, <http://www.aph.gov.au/hansard/ reps/dailys/dr070807.pdf>

Parsons, W. 1995, *Public Policy: An introduction to the theory and practice of policy analysis*, Edward Elgar, Cambridge, UK.

Pearson, N. 2003, *Underlying Principles of a New Policy for the Restoration of Indigenous Social Order*, Cape York Partnerships, viewed 16 May 2010, <http://www.capeyorkpartnerships.com/downloads/noel-pearson-papers/ principles-of-new-policy-for-restoration-of-indigenous-social-order-230703. pdf>

Sackville, R. 1979, *Final Report of the South Australian Royal Commission into the Non-Medical Use of Drugs*, South Australian Government Printer, Adelaide.

10. Expanding the deliberations about the research–policy gap: useful ideas from the literature

Gabriele Bammer, Lyndall Strazdins,
David McDonald, Helen Berry, Alison Ritter,
Peter Deane and Lorrae van Kerkhoff

Introduction

Concern is mounting nationally and globally about the wellbeing of children and young people, with governments under increasing pressure to develop effective policies. There is considerable interest in how researchers can best support policymakers in this enterprise. This chapter presents the results of a reading, discussion and writing group that examined an eclectic range of literature for insights into improving research–policy interactions. The chapter is based on evaluating our experiences in research–policy interactions against ideas generated by reading about 200 books and journal articles.

Each of us is involved in research that seeks to influence policy—in Australia, globally or both—and we have combined forces to strengthen our understanding of how to become more effective in that process. We actively traded ideas between our experiences as researchers, investigating global environmental change and food security (GB, PD), illicit drugs (AR, GB, DM), health-promoting working conditions (LS), mental health and wellbeing (HB) and global public health institutions (LvK). Some of us (AR, HB, DM) have had previous careers as public servants.

There is now a very large literature about research–policy interactions, but there have been few attempts to draw it together in any systematic way, especially in terms of marrying insights across different areas such as environment and population health. We read in both of these areas on the assumption that expanding the range of considerations would open up new ideas and issues for debate about research–policy interactions. There are many ways in which we could have proceeded. To draw on the group's strength in representing a diversity of research interests, as well as policymaking experience, we chose an expansive literature survey encompassing

1) how research is used to support policymaking

2) evaluating research–policy interactions

3) a range of considerations about the research enterprise, including quality, scope and capacity.

We focus particularly on the research role of providing technical support and differentiate this into two components: the extent and quality of the technical support (the amount of research information that is available and its validity), and the process through which technical support is provided. We do not explore the role of research in evaluating government policy or in providing new social theory, ideas and critique; nor do we explore debates about scientific knowledge (for example, Godfrey-Smith 2003; Jasanoff 1998; Redclift 1998). We also do not deal with insights from theories of policymaking, which highlight different aspects of a messy and complex process. Thus, we largely exclude issues of power and pressure groups, as well as opportunistic responses when policy windows open. We have dealt with these issues elsewhere (Ritter and Bammer, 2010).

We have two overall aims in this chapter. One is to present a number of interesting ideas that emerged from our reading and discussion and that could assist researchers and policymakers to improve their interactions. The second is to highlight aspects of this connection that would benefit from further investigation. We believe that there is much to be gained from research targeted at better understanding the research–policy nexus itself. The next section in this chapter provides selections from the current literature on research–policy interactions. We then deal with two significant gaps in some detail: lack of evaluation and lack of consideration of key aspects of the research enterprise.

Selected literature on research–policy interactions

Our reading identified a number of key reviews (for example, Bulmer 1986; Edwards 2001; Hanney et al. 2003; Nutley et al. 2007) and while our considerations intersect with theirs, we seek to complement rather than replicate their analyses. We also acknowledge that we will have missed key references and that the English-language literature we read—mostly from the United States, the United Kingdom, Australia and Canada—is not representative of research–policy interactions globally.

We found a large literature exhorting researchers to conduct investigations that are more relevant to policy concerns (for example, Edwards 2004; Gregrich

2003), along with many papers urging researchers to pay more conscious attention to the presentation of research results, especially writing short reports tailored to policymakers, abridging results without oversimplification and taking care that they reach policymakers through targeted approaches, such as special mailings or face-to-face presentations (for example, Brownson et al. 2006; Edwards 2004; Heyman 2000; Saunders 2006; Secker 1993). We begin our considerations by examining literature that views researchers and policymakers as 'two communities' (Booth 1988), seeing the primary task of engagement as bridging these communities. We consider the different perspectives of policymakers and researchers, different kinds of interaction between these two groups, questions and check lists that aim to alert researchers to key issues relevant to influencing policy and ways of spanning the boundaries. We also look at the value of highlighting rather than glossing over the heterogeneity within each community.

Different perspectives of researchers and policymakers

The 'two-communities' approach raises awareness of the different perspectives of policymakers and researchers, which can make working together difficult. Gregrich (2003) emphasised

- different research and policy priorities, so that research does not address the most urgent questions for policymakers

- inability on each side to effectively manage uncertainties, plus lack of understanding of the limitations inherent in research and policy approaches

- inability to communicate vital information to the 'other side'

- different time cycles, so that, for example, release of research findings rarely takes into consideration the policymakers' decision-making timelines, such as budget and legislative cycles

- lack of researcher appreciation of policy funding constraints

- no current differentiation of researchers from self-interested parties seeking to influence public policy.

Heyman (2000) has taken a different approach, highlighting

- researcher emphasis on making one change at a time and holding other variables constant versus policymaker emphasis on multiple changes and horse-trading between options

- researcher emphasis on randomised controlled trials as a gold standard versus the political difficulties of running trials on social policies; voters expect policies to be based on the best evidence rather than experimentation, which can succeed or fail

- researcher emphasis on central tendency (such as effects of interventions on mean scores) versus policymaker emphasis on the full diversity of the effects of policy

- researcher dismissal of 'outliers' versus policymaker attraction to unusual stories that can encapsulate symbolic power and/or capture the media

- researcher emphasis on targeting for maximum benefit versus policymaker emphasis on general applicability

- researcher emphasis on long-term effectiveness versus policymaker favouring of short-term results that fit within budgetary, electoral or other politically significant cycles.

Gibson (2003a, 2003b) provided a complementary analysis to those of Gregrich and Heyman, exploring a matrix between the 'irrefutability' of the evidence and the 'immutability' of policy (Table 10.1). Changed, or new, policy is most likely when the evidence for change is strong and the political forces maintaining the existing policy are weak. Changed policy is least likely when the evidence is weak and the political forces maintaining the existing policy are strong. When the evidence for change is strong, and the political forces maintaining the existing policy are also strong, the stage is set for confrontation. Nathan and colleagues (2005) made the same point when they said '[w]here strong interests and powerful groups oppose policy direction, the evidence base for government action…needs to be substantial'.

Table 10.1 Likelihood of change

		Irrefutability of the evidence	
		High	*Low*
Immutability of the policy	*High*	Confrontation	Change very unlikely
	Low	Change likely	No pressure for change

Note: The likelihood of change depends on the strength of competition between political forces seeking to maintain existing policy ('immutability of the policy') and research evidence about the need for change ('irrefutability of the evidence').

Adapted from Gibson (2003b).

Gibson (2003b:26) went on to explore the considerations that influence policymakers in such circumstances and posited five indicators of their likely responsiveness to research

1. Responsibility—'The extent to which the policy-making organisation is unequivocally responsible for the policy problem, either in terms of legislative requirements or precedent established by prior action.' The more responsible they are, the more likely they are to act.

2. Capacity—'The extent to which the policy-making organisation has the capacity and power to effect change in the problem.'

3. Performance—'The extent to which it is possible to measure the policy-making organisation's performance in relation to the policy problem.'

4. '"Theatre of justification"—The extent to which performance information and other data relevant to the problem are available for public scrutiny and debate.' In other words, the more the public can see and is interested in whether or not research results are being taken into account, the more likely policymakers are to be responsive to research.

5. 'Vulnerability to the consequences of error—The extent to which there is a cost (political or economic) for policy failure. Research responsiveness will increase as these costs increase.'

Gibson also pointed out that it is simplistic to think of research being *translated* into policy, as if it were a process of converting words from one language to another. Instead, he argued that the process is more accurately thought of as *transformation*, with the policy process absorbing and reconstituting the research to meet its own goals (Gibson 2003a, 2003b).

One way to deal with the differences in perspectives between researchers and policymakers is for closer connection between them. We turn to this literature now.

Connecting researchers and policymakers

In seeking to better understand different ways in which researchers and policymakers can connect, it is useful first to present published models. Jones and Seelig (2004) provided a typology differentiating between 'engineering', 'engagement' and 'enlightenment' models of research–policy interaction. The *engineering model* assumes a rational process in which the role of science is to provide conclusive evidence. Researchers are the technical experts who generate a solution to the problem identified and defined by policy, without questioning or involvement in policy goals or in the way knowledge is received or implemented. (This leaves aside considerations of the limited circumstances in which research can in fact provide *conclusive* evidence.) An *engagement model* takes this one step further. Rather than just being an evidence provider, the researcher is committed to bringing the knowledge, skills and values of their research to influence policy. The researcher takes a more hands-on approach, seeking and building collaborative relationships with relevant policymakers, so that their input and evidence can influence policy directly. The third model—the *enlightenment model*—is essentially one of no engagement, in which researchers are neither service providers nor collaborators, but are focused on their particular investigative enterprise. The policy influence of their work is not managed; the research might eventually influence policy through diffusion, but intellectual independence and excellence are the priorities. As this typology demonstrates, researchers can take different stances to their interaction with policymakers. While individual researchers' approaches will not always fit neatly into one of these boxes, it is useful to understand these positions, as promoting a particular type of connection can clash with the stance of the researcher and therefore be resisted.

The 'engagement model' has gained increasing popularity, with a growing literature suggesting not only how research might influence policy, but also how policy might affect research. This literature promotes greater involvement of policymakers earlier in the research process to enhance the relevance of the research (Walter et al. 2005) and advocates close working partnerships that span the whole research process (Brownson et al. 2006). Such engagement starts with the recognition that the research–policy nexus is not an 'input-output relationship (research in and policy out)' (Edwards 2004:5), but is complex and iterative. Key tasks are to jointly define the problem and to provide ways for policymakers to gain a deep understanding of research findings. The latter can include, for example, building models that allow policymakers to examine hypothetically the consequences of different policy options through various future scenarios (Henrichs 2006).

A related literature concerns adaptive management—an influential approach in the environmental sciences that has, as yet, had little impact in the areas of health and wellbeing. While care must be taken in pulling a theorisation from one field to another—as the premises of the originating theory might not apply in the new field—adaptive management can have broad value, as it addresses the common inability for research to be able to provide conclusive evidence, especially on complex problems. It seeks to guide policymaking in conditions in which significant uncertainties remain. It emphasises learning from experience and from evolving knowledge. In other words, the aim is for policymakers to try new approaches and to continually modify them based on what happens and on new developments in research. As Cash and Moser (2000:117) pointed out for policymaking on environmental issues, '[t]he central notion of this perspective is that for environmental risks characterized by long time horizons and high levels of uncertainty and stochasticity [lacking any predictable order], effective policy should be based on adaptive, iterative, and flexible experimentation'.

In terms of child and youth health, the area of child protection is one that could potentially benefit from an adaptive management approach. Child protection is complex and there is no clear evidence of the best ways forward. Adaptive management emphasises high levels of communication and information flow, the creation of integrated information and decision systems and a process that builds trust through participation, learning and iteration (Cash and Moser 2000). Despite its appeal, there are also significant challenges, as Kasperson (2008) has pointed out. These include the likelihood of eroding public confidence, as well as policy and research credibility, through open acknowledgment of high uncertainty or past errors. In addition, mid-course corrections can raise questions about competence.

For researchers and policymakers trying to improve their interactions, these insights raise important questions that signal the need for a shared dialogue, and that show where further research would be useful. They also help avoid simplistic thinking about what might be involved in research–policy engagement. In the next section, we provide two sets of questions to guide thinking about the interactions between researchers and policymakers.

Questions and checklists

A helpful facet of the research–policy interactions literature is sets of questions and checklists that aim to help researchers build an effective exchange with policymakers. Along with providing an analytical framework for understanding the complexities of interacting with policymakers, they provide strategies for effective connections. We present two excellent examples here.

The first is a set of questions developed by Jones and Seelig (2004), which builds on their typology presented above. We have modified the questions to use child and youth health and wellbeing as the example. The value of the questions is that they alert researchers to the political and research contexts in which they and the policymakers are operating, the extent to which research informs policy in the area of interest and the types of connections between researchers and policymakers that are standard in that area. These could help researchers tailor their efforts to achieve greater influence, as researchers will be more likely to persuade policymakers if they can: 1) demonstrate understanding of how research informs policy in a particular content area; and 2) show sensitivity to the political context in which the policymakers operate. The questions are as follows

• What does it mean to link research and policy in considerations of the health and wellbeing of children and young people?

- In which countries is this prominent on the policy agenda? Why or why not? In which regional and global bodies is it prominent on the policy agenda? Why or why not?

- Nationally and internationally, what are the main drivers of the idea of research-informed policy on the health and wellbeing of children and young people in the early twenty-first century? What have they been in recent decades?

- Why is policy interested in this topic now and how strong is this interest? Do policymakers in the various jurisdictions have similar or different interests in this issue?

- Which model(s) (engineering, engagement or enlightenment) best describes the current research–policy relationship and expectations for this relationship?

- Is there consensus between researchers and policymakers on the best model?

- What other relationships are possible and desirable?

- Are there any risks to manage?

- Which model(s) would be optimal? Is there a preferred model? Why or why not?

Second, Court and Young (2006:88) have developed a matrix of questions and suggestions for researchers seeking to influence policy. These are presented in Table 10.2—again adapted for the area of child and youth wellbeing.

Boundary spanners and boundary organisations

There is another literature that posits that connections between researchers and policymakers can be strengthened if this becomes a specific task for selected individuals and/or organisations. This is also one response to the question of who is responsible for feeding research into the policy mix and how. Various terms have been used to describe this task when it is undertaken by individuals, including 'boundary spanner' (Williams 2002), 'research retailer' (Lomas 1993) and 'knowledge broker' (Dobbins et al. 2009). Boundary spanners tend to work with a high degree of autonomy, are negotiators and brokers comfortable with complex, ambiguous situations and perform 'the role of "policy entrepreneur" to connect problems to solutions, and mobilize resources and effort in the search for successful outcomes' (Williams 2002:121). Detailed examples of people who have effectively filled this role are, however, rare. The chapters by Humphreys and Vines, Goldfeld and Neuhauser in this volume begin to fill this gap.

In terms of boundary organisations, Rayner (2006) has argued for new institutional forms to bring science and policy together. These should also include representation of broader public viewpoints. In particular, he advocated 'flexible, reflexive, and accountable institutions of representative democracy that can track the emergence of issues, and are imbued with regulatory authority to respond proportionately as new information develops' (Rayner 2006:6). He went on to say that 'if we recognize that science cannot compel public policy, the need to develop effective institutional arrangements for it to appropriately inform public policy is greater than ever' (Rayner 2006:6). Van Kerkhoff (2008) made a similar argument. The Australian Research Alliance for Children and Youth (ARACY) is an example of such a boundary organisation, with the chapter by Sanson and Stanley in this volume outlining how it operates in this capacity.

Consideration of boundaries also refocuses attention away from demarcation of different research and policy roles towards 'the blurring of boundaries' in propelling more meaningful research–policy interactions (Guston 2001:399). This line of inquiry could profitably lead into considerations of co-production of science and policy (Jasanoff 1996; Lövbrand 2007; St Clair 2006), but we do not follow it here.

Adding complexity to the 'two communities'

While the two-communities framing of the research–policy relationship alerts each 'side' to the interests and perspectives of the other, it glosses over the heterogeneity within each group. When researchers and policymakers better understand the diversity in the 'other side', they can more effectively target their interaction efforts and enhance understanding of their potential partners. For example, researchers need to understand when they can be most effective targeting politicians versus public servants, as well as whether the national, state or local level is appropriate. On the other hand, policymakers seeking to commission confidential research into politically sensitive areas could benefit from knowing that university-based researchers are likely to want to publish the results of any studies they undertake, whereas this will be less of a concern for consultancy-based researchers. We now briefly outline the different types of members in each group.

Researchers are differentiated by the settings in which they work and the motivations for their investigations. Settings include universities, public-sector think tanks, private think tanks, non-governmental organisations and consultancy firms. Researchers can also work in-house for government departments and business research and development departments. They can also have a range of motivations for their research, including being curiosity driven, in other words, pursuing knowledge for its own sake; following their own agendas; and undertaking research that meets the particular needs of their employers. Each of these is likely to lead to a different orientation to policymaking.

Similarly, if we look at a national level, government policymakers can be categorised as elected, appointed and career officials. In a democracy such as Australia, for example, elected officials can be further differentiated between politicians in power, those in major opposition parties and those in minor parties (who could be influential if they hold the balance of power). Appointed officials include political advisers and heads of government departments. Career officials are public servants whose position continues regardless of which government is in power. Some are deeply knowledgeable about a particular policy area, while others have more generalist and less contextualised policymaking skills. Different levels of government provide another layer of diversity in numbers, types and power of policymakers. This diversity becomes particularly significant for regional and global issues. It is also worth noting that policymakers are 'elusive as a category' (Crewe and Young 2002:5). As these authors point out, apart from those in the most senior positions, government officials often do not think of themselves as policymakers, but instead see themselves as trying to influence those higher up.

The topics discussed to this point give a flavour of the sorts of issues covered in the research–policy interactions literature. We have also highlighted one limitation, which is the lack of detailed consideration given to heterogeneity among researchers and policymakers and their respective contexts. We now move on to discuss two other sets of limitations. First, we explore the general lack of, and difficulties in, the evaluation of research–policy interactions. Second, we explore a number of aspects of research that, we suggest, need closer attention.

Evaluating research–policy interactions

We found little evidence about evaluation of the effectiveness of research support for policymaking, suggesting that there is inadequate learning about what works best, why and in which situations. We are not alone in these concerns. A wide-ranging and in-depth review of literature and case studies conducted for a UK government agency reported: 'The case studies revealed no examples of rigorous evaluation of the organisations' practices to maximise research impact. For the most part…sources base their conclusions upon self-reporting by and observation of participants in the research–practice relationship' (Nutley et al. 2003:16).

What do we mean by evaluation? A UN definition emphasises 'expected and achieved accomplishments, examining the results chain, processes, contextual factors and causality, in order to understand achievements or the lack thereof' (United Nations Evaluation Group 2005:5). Both process and outcomes are important. To markedly improve our understanding of research–policy interactions, it is important to evaluate a range of issues, including: 1) the amount and quality of the research evidence provided; 2) the processes involved in developing and implementing research support for policy decision making; 3) the utilisation of research support by people engaged in decision-making activity; and 4) the impact of the research support on policy activity and stakeholders, and on the researchers themselves.

In principle, evaluation can take different forms at the various stages of a research–policy interaction, serving different purposes. Formative evaluation occurs early in the process to assess if the benefits of providing research support for policy are likely to justify the expenditures of time, money and expertise required (European Commission 2001). Such evaluation contributes to the development and finetuning of the interaction, clarifying and joining up goals, resources, activities, products and hoped-for outcomes. Formative evaluation is context specific and usually provides little information that can be generalised. Summative evaluation, on the other hand, is conducted after the research–policy interaction has been operating for some time or has concluded. It provides information on what has been achieved and how. It should demonstrate how the outputs and outcomes are causally related to the activities undertaken. Summative evaluation provides information that can be used to make decisions about future research–policy interactions. For example, it can reveal whether the research quality was adequate, and whether continuing interactions should continue unchanged, continue in a different form or be terminated.

In practice, however, evaluating the effectiveness of research–policy interactions is not a simple or straightforward task. For example, if such evaluation involves researchers or research organisations that are actively seeking to make policy links, the assessment has to serve multiple goals. These include demonstrating success, process accountability, return on investment, building or maintaining credibility as well as fostering strategic planning and efforts to improve.

To use evaluation effectively for accountability, we need better understanding of the complexities of research–policy interactions, so that any evaluation can take these into account in an appropriate manner. This will also assist in enhancing learning and improving future performance. Furthermore, the increasing demands of decision makers for near to 'real-time' evaluative information provides a challenge to the evaluation profession that has, in the past, concentrated on relatively lengthy evaluation research that has frequently delivered findings too late to be of use (Rist and Stame 2006).

Table 10.2 Questions and suggestions for researchers aiming to influence policy

	What you need to know	What you need to do	How to do it
Political context	• Who are the policymakers? • Is there policymaker demand for new ideas? • What are the sources/strengths of resistance? • What is the policymaking process? • What are the opportunities and timing for input into formal processes?	• Get to know the policymakers, their agendas and their constraints. • Identify potential supporters and opponents. • Keep an eye on the horizon and prepare for opportunities in regular policy processes. • Look out for—and react to—unexpected policy 'windows'.	• Work with the policymakers. • Seek commissions. • Line up research programs with high-profile policy events. • Reserve resources to be able to move quickly to respond to policy windows. • Allow sufficient time and resources.
Evidence	• What is the current theory? • What are the prevailing narratives? • How divergent is the new evidence? • What sort of evidence will convince policymakers?	• Establish credibility over the long term. • Provide practical solutions to problems. • Establish legitimacy. • Build a convincing case and present clear policy options. • Package new ideas in familiar theory or narratives. • Communicate effectively.	• Build up programs of high-quality work. • Action research and pilot projects to demonstrate benefits of new approaches. • Use participatory approaches to help with legitimacy and implementation. • Have clear strategies and resources for communication from the start. • Face-to-face communication.
Links	• Who are the key stakeholders in the policy discourse? • What links and networks exist between them? • Who are the intermediaries and what influence do they have? • Whose side are they on?	• Get to know the other stakeholders. • Establish a presence in existing networks. • Build coalitions with like-minded stakeholders. • Build new policy networks.	• Create partnerships between researchers, policymakers and communities. • Identify key networkers and salespeople. • Use informal contacts.
External Influences	• Who are main national and international actors in the policy process? • What influence do they have? • What are their action priorities? • What are their research priorities and mechanisms?	• Get to know the main actors, their priorities and constraints. • Identify potential supporters, key individuals and networks. • Establish credibility. • Keep an eye on policies of the main actors and look out for policy windows.	• Develop extensive background on main actors' policies. • Orient communications to suit main actors' priorities and language. • Try to work with the main actors and seek commissions. • Contact (regularly) key individuals.

Adapted from Court and Young (2006:88).

Limitations of the research enterprise

Considerations of research–policy interactions tend to focus on the process of providing research for policymaking, rather than the quality of the research, research capacity or other salient issues on the research side of the equation. In this section, we start to tease out some of these issues. We begin with the limitations of what research can offer, particularly in terms of decreasing uncertainty. We then deal with the lack of uniform quality standards and finish by considering limitations in research capacity.

Research can increase rather than decrease uncertainty

Rayner (2006) reminded us that the promise that research can point to clear-cut policy options is often illusory. While his comments focused on environmental risk, they are equally true in other areas, such as child and youth wellbeing. As he pointed out:

> [P]olicy makers are consistently led to believe that, given time and money, scientific inquiry will reduce relevant uncertainty about environmental risk. Their scientific advisors hold out the promise that more fine-grained information will clarify the nature and extent of the problem and enable policy makers to craft efficient and effective responses.

He went on to say that this disregards two factors—namely, that increased research knowledge often raises new questions leading to new uncertainties and that more knowledge can lead to more conflicting views. In both cases, the evidence base for policy becomes less rather than more secure (Rayner 2006:5).

For example, the statistics show that many abused and neglected children have mothers dependent on illicit drugs. Nevertheless, research has also shown that many of these mothers go to great lengths to shield their children from the effects of their drug use (Richter and Bammer 2000) and that drug-dependent mothers are judged more harshly by society—and themselves—than other mothers, even when their behaviour is very similar (Banwell and Bammer 2006). We also know that removing children from abusive family situations can have both beneficial and harmful effects. The more research delves into this area, the less clear the way to intervene becomes.

Lack of uniform quality standards

As more research is undertaken and as the problems addressed become more complex, requiring an array of research knowledge, it becomes harder to compile, let alone critically review, what is known. A streamlined systematic review process has been successfully introduced for judging medical research through the Cochrane Collaboration (n.d.) and for social, behavioural and education research through the Campbell Collaboration (n.d.). Another outstanding example comes from the environmental area where the Intergovernmental Panel on Climate Change (IPCC 2008) has a strenuous vetting process for research evidence. Such processes are, however, very expensive and are not applied uniformly to all areas of research.

This leads us to a more general discussion of criteria for judging research. In Australia, the National Health and Medical Research Council (NHMRC 2000) evaluated four dimensions: level (study design); quality (bias); relevance (applicability to policy); and strength (precision, reproducibility and attributability). Jacobs and colleagues (2005) put forward most of the same factors, as well as some additional ones. They suggested that usefulness could be judged by assessing whether researchers are asking and answering the 'right' questions, whether decision makers are able to understand the data and analyses, whether the findings are considered accurate, trustworthy and relevant to the decision that has to be made, whether the information is timely and whether the findings are sensitive to relevant constraints. Cash et al. (2003) reiterated some of these issues and gave additional emphasis to legitimacy— in other words, inclusive, respectful and fair treatment of diverse stakeholder values and perspectives.

A key point here is that not all research deserves to influence policy. This is not sufficiently acknowledged when researchers are encouraged to engage with policymakers. For example, research that takes a narrowly focused, simplistic view of a complex problem, which is self-serving self-promotion or which is simply poorly conceived and executed might best be disregarded. We argue that the onus is on the research community, rather than the policy community, to effectively screen research. The processes used by the IPCC and Cochrane and Campbell Collaborations, as well as the more general criteria for judging research, provide guidance on how this can be done. (We note, however, that over-emphasis on one criterion for judging quality—such as reliance on randomised controlled trials in the case of the Cochrane Collaboration—can lead to its own problems. For other challenges raised by reviews, see Pawson 2002a, 2002b.)

Limitations to research capacity

As well as restrictions on what research can achieve in producing certainty, research capacity is also inherently limited. In his book *Inquiry and Change* (1990:162), Charles Lindblom contended that '[p]rofessional inquiry is a scarce resource even in a wealthy US, never abundant enough to permit study of all important social phenomena and problems, even if the entire adult population became social scientists'. He reminded us, more generally, that there can never be enough researchers to study all the important problems existing at any one time.

We have noted that not all research deserves to influence policy. Lindblom took this further, highlighting various research behaviours and institutional structures that limit the value of research. These include researcher difficulties in remaining open to new ideas that challenge key beliefs, hasty work because of competition, insulation through institutionalised subfields (often referred to as a silo mentality), allowing available research methods to dictate the work rather than the requirements of the problem and bypassing troublesome topics in favour of easier ones. These problems are all relevant to the field of child and youth wellbeing, where causal pathways and outcomes are complex. The temptation can be to conduct research on narrow topics and to 'de-contextualise' the investigation, ignoring the importance of particular social, cultural and familial structures. The findings of such studies can be quite misleading for policy development.

While the focus here has been mostly on Australia, it is also worth remembering that research capacity, in terms of the number of researchers, is unevenly distributed globally. As Anderson and Bammer (2005) have shown, it is greatly skewed in favour of high-income countries. For example, they report that United Nations Educational, Scientific and Cultural Organisation (UNESCO) Research and Development data (1996–2002) show that there is a median of 2618 researchers per million inhabitants in upper-income economy countries compared with 47 in low-income economy countries. (While these figures starkly illustrate the disparity, the exact numbers must be treated with caution, as UNESCO provided data for only 91 of the world's 241 countries and for many of the 91 countries some data are missing.)

Limitations in capacity raise questions about what research should be given priority, and this is relevant in both high and low-income countries.

The issue of research priorities also highlights a more practical query about which sorts of research are of value to policymakers and whether these are available to them. There is a general view that policymakers look for summaries, reviews and 'trans-disciplinary' analyses that include economic modelling, meta-analysis and an understanding of human behaviour (Davies 2004). Compelling stories that encapsulate the findings in terms of impact on an individual or family can also be very powerful. This does not, however, seem to be an area that has attracted much empirical research—Ritter's (2008) investigation of Australian policymakers in the area of illicit drugs is an exception—so that there could be benefit in further investigation of what policymakers need to work effectively and how easy it is for them to access.

Conclusions

The central argument of this chapter is that considerations of research–policy interactions have been too narrow and that broadening the focus raises critical questions that have yet to receive the attention they warrant. We have illustrated this by bringing together literature from the fields of environment and population health, as well as from three areas that are generally treated separately: research–policy interactions, their evaluation and considerations of research amount and quality. Gone are the days when researchers gloried in the 'practical uselessness' of their investigations (Passmore 1978). There are, however, not yet well thought through approaches to how research can best support policymaking, particularly policymaking that seeks to respond to complex social problems. The profound challenges posed by considerations of the wellbeing of children and young people highlight this need and provide a stimulus for action. Our focus here has been on both providing available knowledge to stimulate new thinking about research–policy interactions and encouraging more research, reflection and documentation of these interactions. We want to encourage others to take a broad view and to join us in examining and debating key issues of research priorities, research limitations and how researchers can best provide technical support for policy.

Acknowledgments

This chapter is based on an unpublished report written for the Global Environmental Change and Food Systems Project (<www.gecafs.org>), which was funded from the UK Natural Environment Research Council's support for that project. The work of the reading group was also supported by the Colonial Foundation Trust through the Drug Policy Modelling Program. Valuable comments on earlier drafts were provided by Doctors Polly Ericksen, John Ingram and Alice Roughley. Professor Dorothy Broom contributed to the early phase of the group's reading and discussion.

References

Anderson, C. and Bammer, G. 2005, 'Measuring the global research environment: information science challenges for the 21st century', *Sparking Synergies: Bringing research and practice together. Proceedings of the 68th American Society of Information Science and Technology Annual Meeting*, Charlotte, NC, 28 October – 2 November 2005, viewed 16 May 2010, <http://eprints.rclis.org/4992/1/Anderson_Measuring.pdf>

Banwell, C. and Bammer, G. 2006, 'Maternal habits: narratives of mothering, social position and drug use', *International Journal of Drug Policy*, vol. 17, pp. 504–13.

Booth, T. 1988, *Developing Policy Research*, Gower Publishing Company, Aldershot, UK.

Brownson, R. C., Royer, C., Ewing, R. and McBride, T. D. 2006, 'Researchers and policymakers: travellers in parallel universes', *American Journal of Preventive Medicine*, vol. 30, no. 2, pp. 164–72.

Bulmer, M. 1986, *Social Science and Social Policy*, Allen & Unwin, London.

Campbell Collaboration n.d., viewed 9 August 2007, <www.campbellcollaboration.org>

Cash, D. W. and Moser, S. C. 2000, 'Linking global and local scales: designing dynamic assessment and management processes', *Global Environmental Change*, vol. 10, no. 2, pp. 109–20.

Cash, D. W., Clark, W. C., Alcock, F., Dickson, N. M., Eckley, N., Guston, D. H., Jager, J. and Mitchell, R. B. 2003, 'Knowledge systems for sustainable development', *Proceedings of the National Academy of Sciences of the United States of America*, vol. 100, no. 14, pp. 8086–91.

Cochrane Collaboration n.d., viewed 9 August 2007, <www.cochrane.org>

Court, J. and Young, J. 2006, 'Bridging research and policy in international development: an analytical and practical framework', *Development in Practice*, vol. 16, no. 1, pp. 85–90.

Crewe, E. and Young, J. 2002, *Bridging research and policy: context, evidence and links*, Working Paper 173, Overseas Development Institute, London, viewed 15 May 2010, <http://www.odi.org.uk/resources/download/151.pdf>

Davies, P. 2004, 'Sociology and policy science: just in time?', *The British Journal of Sociology*, vol. 55, no. 3, pp. 447–50.

Dobbins, M., Robeson, P., Ciliska, D., Hanna, S., Cameron, R., O'Mara, L., Decorby, K. and Mercer, S. 2009, 'A description of a knowledge broker role implemented as part of a randomized controlled trial evaluating three knowledge translation strategies', *Implementation Science*, vol. 4, <http://www.implementationscience.com/content/4/1/23>

Edwards, M. 2001, *Social Policy, Public Policy: From problem to practice*, Allen & Unwin, Crows Nest, NSW.

Edwards, M. 2004, *Social science research and public policy: narrowing the divide*, Occasional Paper 2/2004, Academy of the Social Sciences in Australia, Canberra, viewed 16 May 2010, <http://www.assa.edu.au/publications/occasional_papers/2004_No2.php>

European Commission 2001, *Ex Ante Evaluation: A practical guide for preparing proposals for expenditure programmes*, European Commission, Brussels, viewed 16 May 2010, <http://ec.europa.eu/budget/library/documents/evaluation/guides/ex_ante_guide_2001_en.pdf>

Gibson, B. 2003a, From transfer to transformation: rethinking the relationship between research and policy, PhD Thesis, The Australian National University, Canberra, viewed 1 August 2008, <http://thesis.anu.edu.au/uploads/approved/adt-ANU20040528.165124/public/02whole.pdf>

Gibson, B. 2003b, 'Beyond "two communities"', in V. Lin and B. Gibson (eds), *Evidence-Based Health Policy. Problems and possibilities*, Oxford University Press, UK, pp. 18–30.

Godfrey-Smith, P. 2003, *Theory and Reality: An introduction to the philosophy of science*, University of Chicago Press, Ill.

Gregrich, R. J. 2003, 'A note to researchers: communicating science to policy makers and practitioners', *Journal of Substance Abuse Treatment*, vol. 25, no. 3, pp. 233–7.

Guston, D. 2001, 'Boundary organizations in environmental policy and science: an introduction', *Science, Technology and Human Values*, vol. 26, no. 4, pp. 399–408.

Hanney, S., Gonzalez-Block, M., Buxton, M. J. and Kogan, M. 2003, 'The utilisation of health research in policy-making: concepts, examples and methods of assessment', *Health Research Policy and Systems*, vol. 1, no. 2.

Henrichs, T. 2006, *On the role of scenarios in GECAFS decision-support*, GECAFS Working Paper 4, Global Environmental Change and Food

Systems, Wallingford, UK, viewed 13 February 2007, <http://www.gecafs. org/publications/Publications/GECAFS_Working_Paper_4_Henrichs_ August_2006.pdf>

Heyman, S. J. 2000, 'Health and social policy', in L. F. Berkman and I. Kawachi (eds), *Social Epidemiology*, Oxford University Press, New York, pp. 368–82.

Intergovernmental Panel on Climate Change (IPCC) 2008, 'Procedures for the preparation, review, acceptance, adoption, approval and publication of IPCC reports', Appendix A to the *Principles Governing IPCC Work*, Intergovernmental Panel on Climate Change, Geneva, viewed 18 May 2010, <http://www.ipcc.ch/pdf/ipcc-principles/ipcc-principles-appendix-a.pdf>

Jacobs, K., Garfin, G. and Lenart, M. 2005, 'More than just talk: connecting science and decisionmaking', *Environment: Science and Policy for Sustainable Development*, vol. 47, no. 9, pp. 6–21.

Jasanoff, S. 1996, 'Beyond epistemology: relativism and engagement in the politics of science', *Social Studies of Science*, vol. 26, no. 2, pp. 393–418.

Jasanoff, S. 1998, 'Coming of age in science and technology studies', *Science Communication*, vol. 20, no. 1, pp. 91–8.

Jones, A. and Seelig, T. 2004, *Understanding and enhancing research–policy linkages in Australian housing: a discussion paper*, Australian Housing and Urban Research Institute, Brisbane, viewed 13 February 2007, <http://www. ahuri.edu.au/publications/download.asp?ContentID=20216_pp>

Kasperson, R. E. 2008, 'Coping with deep uncertainty: challenges for environmental assessment and decision making', in G. Bammer and M. Smithson (eds), *Uncertainty and Risk: Multidisciplinary perspectives*, Earthscan, London, pp. 337–47, [extracted in R. E. Kasperson 2008, 'Coping with deep uncertainty', *Integration Insights*, no. 9 (June), viewed 19 May 2010, <http://i2s.anu.edu.au/sites/default/files/integration-insights/ integration-insight_9.pdf>].

Lindblom, C. E. 1990, *Inquiry and Change. The troubled attempt to understand and shape society*, Yale University Press/Russell Sage, New York.

Lomas, J. 1993, 'Retailing research: increasing the role of evidence in clinical services for childbirth', *Milbank Quarterly*, vol. 71, no. 3, pp. 439–75.

Lövbrand, E. 2007, 'Pure science or policy involvement? Ambiguous boundary-work for Swedish carbon cycle science', *Environmental Science and Policy*, vol. 10, no. 1, pp. 39–47.

Nathan, S. A., Develin, E., Grove, N. and Zwi, A. B. 2005, 'An Australian childhood obesity summit: the role of data and evidence in "public" policy making', *Australia & New Zealand Health Policy*, vol. 2:17, viewed 11 February 2007, <http://www.anzhealthpolicy.com/content/pdf/1743-8462-2-17.pdf>

National Health and Medical Research Council (NHMRC) 2000, *How to Use the Evidence: Assessment and application of scientific evidence*, Handbook Series on Preparing Clinical Practice Guidelines, National Health and Medical Research Council, Canberra, viewed 18 May 2010, <http://www.nhmrc.gov.au/_files_nhmrc/file/publications/synopses/cp69.pdf>

Nutley, S., Percy-Smith, J. and Solesbury, W. 2003, 'Models of research impact: a cross-sector review of literature and practice', *Building Effective Literature No. 4*, Learning and Skills Research Centre, London, viewed 18 May 2010, <https://crm.lsnlearning.org.uk/user/order.aspx?code=031418>

Nutley, S. M., Walter, I. and Davies, H. T. O. 2007, *Using Evidence: How research can inform public services*, Policy Press, Bristol.

Passmore, J. 1978, *Science and Its Critics*, Duckworth, London.

Pawson, R. 2002a, 'Evidence-based policy: in search of a method', *Evaluation*, vol. 8, no. 2, pp. 157–81.

Pawson, R. 2002b, 'Evidence-based policy: the promise of "realist synthesis"', *Evaluation*, vol. 8, no. 3, pp. 340–58.

Rayner, S. 2006, 'What drives environmental policy?', *Global Environmental Change*, vol. 16, no. 1, pp. 4–6.

Redclift, M. 1998, 'Dances with wolves? Interdisciplinary research on the global environment', *Global Environmental Change: Human and Policy Dimensions*, vol. 8, no. 3, pp. 177–82.

Richter, K. and Bammer, G. 2000, 'A hierarchy of strategies heroin-using mothers employ to reduce harm to their children', *Journal of Substance Abuse Treatment*, vol. 19, pp. 403–13.

Rist, R. C. and Stame, N. (eds) 2006, *From Studies to Streams: Managing evaluative systems*, Transaction Publishers, NJ.

Ritter, A. 2008, 'How do drug policy makers access research evidence?', *International Journal of Drug Policy*, vol. 20, no. 1, pp. 70–5.

Ritter, A. and Bammer, G. 2010, 'Models of policy-making and their relevance for drug research', *Drug and Alcohol Review*, vol. 29, no. 4, pp. 352–7.

Saunders, P. 2006, 'Social science and public policy: connecting the ivory tower to the corridors of power', *Dialogue*, vol. 25, no. 2, pp. 70–4.

Secker, A. 1993, 'The policy–research interface: an insider's view', *Addiction 88* (Supplement), pp. 115S–20S.

St Clair, A. 2006, 'Global poverty: the co-production of knowledge and politics', *Global Social Policy*, vol. 6, no. 1, pp. 57–77.

United Nations Evaluation Group 2005, *Norms for Evaluation in the UN System*, United Nations Evaluation Group, New York, viewed 16 May 2010, <http://www.uneval.org/papersandpubs/documentdetail.jsp?doc_id=21>

van Kerkhoff, L. 2008, *Making a Difference: Science, action and integrated environmental research*, Sense Publishers, Rotterdam.

Walter, I., Nutley, S. and Davies, H. 2005, 'What works to promote evidence-based practice', *Evidence & Policy*, vol. 1, no. 3, pp. 335–64.

Williams, P. 2002, 'The competent boundary spanner', *Public Administration*, vol. 80, no. 1, pp. 103–24.

Contributors

Gabriele Bammer

Gabriele Bammer is a professor at the National Centre for Epidemiology and Population Health, ANU College of Medicine, Biology and Environment at The Australian National University and a research fellow at the Program in Criminal Justice Policy and Management at Harvard University's John F. Kennedy School of Government. Her main interest is developing methodologies for enhancing research input into tackling complex real-world problems. Knowledge brokering to bridge the research–policy/practice gap is key, along with synthesis of disciplinary and stakeholder knowledge and comprehensively understanding and managing unknowns. These three domains are the foundations of a new discipline: Integration and Implementation Sciences (see <http://i2s.anu.edu.au>). In 2001, she was the Australian representative on the inaugural Fulbright New Century Scholars Program, which targets 'outstanding research scholars and professionals'. She is editor of *Dealing with Uncertainties in Policing Serious Crime* (2010), co-editor of *Uncertainty and Risk: Multidisciplinary perspectives* (2008) and co-author of *Research Integration Using Dialogue Methods* (2009).

Helen Berry

Helen Berry is Associate Professor and Deputy Director (Research) of the Centre for Research and Action in Public Health at the University of Canberra. She also holds adjunct appointments as Associate Professor at The Australian National University and the University of Newcastle. She is a psychiatric epidemiologist with particular interest in investigating the relationship between social capital and mental health and their shared associations with contemporary issues in health and wellbeing. Recently, Helen has extended this work so as to place these research and policy issues in the context of climate change, particularly its impacts in rural and remote locations. Her work involves the use of advanced statistical modelling techniques to analyse representative data sets and evaluate mental health interventions. With a previous career in executive leadership in the public and non-profit sectors, she has a particular interest in the way in which research and public policymaking can work together. Helen leads collaborations on social capital, mental health and climate change with Australian Government agencies, state and local governments and various universities, including in Vietnam.

Robyn Cummins

Robyn Cummins is the Manager of Information Services at The Spastic Centre in New South Wales. With a background in Information Science, Robyn has been responsible for a number of initiatives that use new web technologies for knowledge sharing, clinical collaboration and to address some of the social and information needs of people with a disability and their families. A strong corporate culture of innovation, with national and international networks, has enabled Robyn and her colleagues to engage in a range of strategic knowledge-brokering activities to a diverse range of stakeholders.

Peter Deane

Peter Deane has a research interest in supra-disciplinarity, particularly inter- and trans-disciplinarity, as part of a response to the socio-ecological challenges arising in modern societies. He works as a research assistant at the National Centre for Epidemiology and Population Health, ANU College of Medicine, Biology and Environment at The Australian National University on the development of Integration and Implementation Sciences. He is co-author of *Research Integration Using Dialogue Methods* (2009).

Meredith Edwards

Meredith Edwards is an Emeritus Professor at the University of Canberra. Her current main research interests are public-sector governance issues, the research–policy relationship and community engagement issues. Her recent major publications can be found online at <www.canberra.edu.au/corpgov-aps>. Although she trained as an economist, throughout her career she has been a lecturer, researcher, policy analyst and administrator working in academia and the public sector. She was the inaugural director of the National Institute for Governance at the University of Canberra in 1999. Meredith is a fellow of the Academy of Social Sciences of Australia, a member of the UN Committee of Experts on Public Administration and has an Order of Australia (AM) for services to education and welfare.

Sharon Goldfeld

Sharon Goldfeld is a paediatrician and public health physician with a PhD in health services research. For the past decade, she has divided her time between the policy, research and clinical worlds as the Principal Medical Advisor in child health to the Victorian Department of Education and Early Childhood Development, a consultant community paediatrician, senior research fellow at the Centre for Community Child Health and senior lecturer at the University of Melbourne. Sharon has a particular interest in children's health services research, data and policy and has spearheaded substantial work in this area including Headline Indicators for Australia's Children and the national roll-out of the Australian Early Development Index. She has been recipient of the prestigious international Harkness Fellowship in healthcare policy and the Aileen Plant Medal for her contribution to public health research. Sharon is a member of several national and state committees that focus on children's issues and has been a passionate advocate for children in both her policy and academic roles.

Brian Head

Brian Head took up a research chair at the University of Queensland in 2007. A political scientist by training, he has held senior roles in government, academia and the non-government sector. From 1990 to 2003, he worked in the Queensland Government, including in senior roles in intergovernmental negotiations, policy development and public-sector reform. From 2003 to 2005, he was a research professor at Griffith University and subsequently completed two years leading the Australian Research Alliance for Children and Youth (ARACY) in Canberra. He is the author and editor of several books on public policy and organisational management issues. His major interests are collaboration, joined-up government, federalism, service delivery, integrity, community consultation, evaluation and evidence-based policy. He is committed to improving linkages between the research sector, the government sector and service providers.

Cathy Humphreys

Cathy Humphreys is the Alfred Felton Chair of Child and Family Welfare—a professorship established in collaboration between the Department of Social Work at the University of Melbourne, the Centre for Excellence for Child and Family Welfare in Victoria (the peak body for child and family welfare agencies) and the Alfred Felton Trust. She was a social work practitioner in the mental health and child and family welfare sector for 16 years before becoming a social work academic with a specialty in research and research utilisation in the domestic violence and child and family practice areas. She worked at the University of New South Wales and the University of Warwick in the United Kingdom before taking up the Chair at the University of Melbourne. The Alfred Felton Research Program has now developed a sustained program of research in the areas of domestic and family violence, out-of-home care and research utilisation.

David McDonald

David McDonald is a social scientist with research interests in integration and evidence-informed public policy, particularly in domains where public health and criminology/criminal justice intersect, such as alcohol, tobacco and other drugs policy. He is the principal of the Canberra-based consultancy Social Research & Evaluation Pty Ltd and is a Visiting Fellow at the National Centre for Epidemiology and Population Health at The Australian National University. He is co-author of *Research Integration Using Dialogue Methods* (2009).

Annette Michaux

Annette Michaux is General Manager, Social Policy and Research, at The Benevolent Society, a large non-profit organisation with the purpose of creating caring and inclusive communities and a just society. Annette's role at The Benevolent Society is to drive the organisation's increasing focus on evidence-informed practice, research and advocacy. A social worker and adult educator by training, Annette has held a number of senior policy and operational positions in government and non-profit organisations. She was the Executive Officer of the NSW Child Protection Council and a member of the senior policy team at the NSW Commission for Children and Young People. Earlier in her career, Annette worked as a child welfare officer and ran a large inner-city community centre in Sydney. She has been on numerous committees and is currently a board member of the Australasian Evaluation Society and a member of the Australian Research Alliance for Children and Youth (ARACY), Future Generations—Network Advisory Committee.

Michael Moore

Michael Moore is the Chief Executive Officer of the Public Health Association of Australia. He is a former Minister of Health and Community Care and was an independent member of the Australian Capital Territory Legislative Assembly for four terms, from 1989 to 2001. He was the first Australian independent member to be appointed as a minister to a government executive. Michael holds a postgraduate diploma in education and a master's degree in population health, is an adjunct professor with the University of Canberra and is widely published. He is also a political and social columnist who has served on a range of boards, including the Australian Health Care Reform Alliance, the National Drug Research Institute and the Institute of Public Administration.

J. Fraser Mustard CC

J. Fraser Mustard CC completed his medical degree in Toronto in 1953, after which he undertook PhD studies in Cambridge focused on the role of platelets in cardiovascular disease. His subsequent 10 years of research in Toronto resulted in a prestigious Gairdner Award. When he moved to McMaster University in 1966 as a founding member of its medical school, he continued his research on platelets and recruited scientists who helped to establish a major centre for thrombosis research. He was also deeply involved in developing the innovative problem-based program of medical education. In 1982, Fraser established the Canadian Institute for Advanced Research. As its president for 14 years, he raised funds and oversaw the formation of interdisciplinary teams of distinguished investigators to explore significant scientific and social challenges. He now heads the Founders' Network, which involves his connections with more than 1000 individuals. He has become a tireless advocate nationally and internationally of the importance of early brain development for health, behaviour, learning and quality of life. Fraser's accomplishments have relied on his energy, vision, insight, leadership ability and establishment of connections, networks and interdisciplinary research. He is a Companion of the Order of Canada.

Linda Neuhauser

Linda Neuhauser is a Clinical Professor of Community Health and Human Development at the University of California, Berkeley School of Public Health. Her research, teaching and practice are focused on translating scientific findings into improved health interventions and policies. She has a particular interest in participatory processes that engage diverse stakeholders to co-design and evaluate large-scale health initiatives. She has more that 100 research and other publications in this area of 'action research'. She is co-principal investigator of the UC Berkeley Health Research for Action Center (<http://www.uchealthaction.org>), which uses participatory processes to investigate health issues and develop health information resources that have now reached more than 30 million households internationally.

Alison Ritter

Alison Ritter is an associate professor at the National Drug and Alcohol Research Centre at the University of New South Wales, and currently directs the Drug Policy Modelling Program. The goal of this program is to advance illicit drug policy through improving the evidence base, developing new policymaking tools and understanding the best mix of policy options. She has a master's degree in clinical psychology and a PhD in psychology. She has worked as a clinical psychologist, conducted clinical research and worked in government. She is a Visiting Fellow at The Australian National University's Regulatory Institutions Network and holds a National Health and Medical Research Council Career Development Award.

Ann Sanson

Ann Sanson is a professor in paediatrics at the University of Melbourne and the Network Coordinator for the Australian Research Alliance for Children and Youth (ARACY). She is a developmental psychologist with particular expertise in longitudinal research; she plays a leading role in the 25-year Australian

Temperament Project and Growing Up in Australia (the Longitudinal Study of Australian Children). Her previous positions include acting director of the Australian Institute of Family Studies and she currently sits on a number of national advisory committees. Her work with ARACY has a strong focus on facilitating knowledge exchange among researchers, policymakers and practitioners in order to promote the wellbeing of children and youth. She is a Fellow of the Australian Psychological Society and has more than 180 publications.

Fiona Stanley AC

Fiona Stanley AC is the Founding Director of the Telethon Institute for Child Health Research, Chair of the Australian Research Alliance for Children and Youth (ARACY) and Professor of the School of Paediatrics and Child Health at the University of Western Australia. Trained in maternal and child health epidemiology and public health, Fiona has spent her career researching the causes of major childhood illnesses such as birth defects. Her research includes the gathering and analysis of population data for epidemiological and public health research; the causes and prevention of birth defects and major neurological disorders, particularly the cerebral palsies; patterns of maternal and child health in Aboriginal and Caucasian populations; various ways of determining the developmental origins of health and disease; collaborations to link research, policy and practice; and strategies to enhance health and wellbeing in populations. Her major contribution has been to establish the Telethon Institute for Child Health Research, a unique multidisciplinary independent research institute focusing on the causes and prevention of major problems affecting children and youth. She has more than 300 publications, books and book chapters and sits on the Prime Minister's Science, Engineering and Innovation Council as well as the Australian Social Inclusion Board. For her research on behalf of Australia's children and Aboriginal social justice, she was named Australian of the Year in 2003 and in 2006 she was made a UNICEF Australia Ambassador for Early Childhood Development.

Lyndall Strazdins

Lyndall Strazdins is a fellow at the National Centre for Epidemiology and Population Health at The Australian National University. Her research addresses current industrial relations changes in the context of an ageing population, intergenerational impacts on children and workforce participation policies. Her research also addresses time pressures and family life, including the impact on health and environmental sustainability. She is an expert advisor for government inquiries and reports.

Lorrae van Kerkhoff

Lorrae van Kerkhoff is a lecturer at the Fenner School of Environment and Society at The Australian National University. Her research interests encompass the role of science in governance, decision and policymaking, including north–south research collaborations, and instruments and processes to foster better relationships between researchers and practitioners. In 2004–05, she was a Fulbright Scholar with the Center for International Development, Harvard University, where she examined the role of research in global public health institutions.

Richard Vines

Richard Vines is Honorary Research Fellow (Professor) at the eScholarship Research Centre structurally located within the library at the University of Melbourne. He is a former quality knowledge manager at the Children's Protection Society in Victoria and 'knowledge broker' with the Centre for Excellence in Child and Family Welfare. In the period 2000–04, he was client manager/consultant to AusIndustry and the Australian Printing Industries Association within the Enhanced Printing Industries Competitiveness Scheme. Subsequent to this, as an independent consultant, he consulted and published extensively about electronic content standards and data interoperability for a wide range of clients. In 2008, Richard was invited to become a foundation member of the Victorian Council of Social Service's Interoperability Working Group. Flowing from the advocacy work of this group, the Victorian Office for the Community Sector has commissioned a number of projects. These have the potential to lay a foundation for reforms associated with the use of semantic publishing and its application to contribute to the dual objectives of minimising undue regulatory burden and enhancing possibilities for cross-domain policy/research/practice coordination.

www.ingramcontent.com/pod-product-compliance
Lightning Source LLC
Chambersburg PA
CBHW061240270326
41927CB00035B/3455